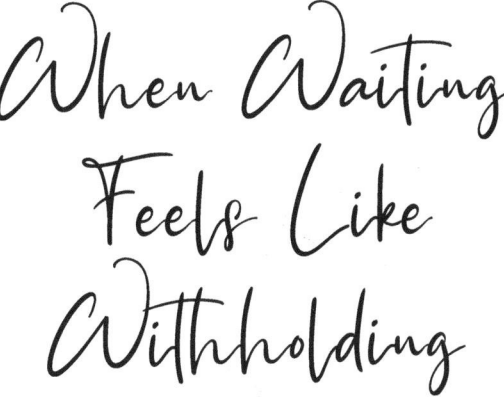

*Trusting God When You
Doubt His Goodness*

JEN ALLEE

ISBN: 978-1-964026-29-9 (paperback)
ISBN: 978-1-964026-30-5 (ebook)

When Waiting Feels Like Withholding
Copyright © 2025 Jen Allee
Cover and interior design Copyright © 2026 Rope Swing Publishing

All rights reserved. Printed in the United States of America. No part of this book may be used or reproduced in any manner whatsoever without written permission from the publisher except in the case of brief quotations embodied in critical articles or reviews. Unless otherwise noted, scripture quotations are taken from the Holy Bible, New International Version®, NIV®. Copyright © 1973, 1978, 1984, 2011 by Biblica, Inc.® Used by permission of Zondervan. All rights reserved worldwide. www.zondervan.com. The "NIV" and "New International Version" are trademarks registered in the United States Patent and Trademark Office by Biblica, Inc.®.

PRESS
AHEAD
PRESS

www.ropeswingpublishing.com

Dedicated to Aaron and Parker
May you always trust His goodness
whenever life finds you waiting.

Table of Contents

Foreword 5

Introduction 7

Section One: The Weight of the Wait

Chapter One: The In-Between 15

Chapter Two: The Partnership 28

Section Two: The Answers We Seek

Chapter Three: Lord, Do You Care? 49

Chapter Four: Can You Help Me Understand? 60

Chapter Five: Have You Forgotten Me? 76

Chapter Six: Are You Punishing Me? 92

Section Three: Moving Forward While Waiting Well

Chapter Seven: Unraveling Your Fixation 115

Chapter Eight: The Benefits of Surrender 133

Chapter Nine: Battling Fear 149

Chapter Ten: The Secret To Perseverance 161

Chapter Eleven: When God Says No 172

Chapter Twelve: When There Is No Bow 191

Chapter Thirteen: The (Real) End 210

Author's Note 228

Acknowledgements 231

About the Author 233

Foreword

Kevin McKee, Lead Pastor, The Chapel, Baton Rouge

When I first encountered Jen Allee, I was struck by her tender way of reflecting on life, especially the difficult seasons she and her husband have walked through. Reading this book brought me back to that moment and reminded me why her voice matters so deeply. As Jen's pastor and a friend of her family, it is a joy and an honor to recommend this book to you.

With honesty and grace, Jen draws on both Scripture and personal experience to describe waiting as "the in-between"—a place between longing and fulfillment. Waiting unsettles us because it leaves us without control, surrounded by uncertainty and silence. Yet throughout the Bible, God consistently uses waiting as a tool to shape His people. As Jen reminds us, waiting is not a mistake; it is a purposeful part of God's work in us.

Through this book, Jen gently shows us that God welcomes our questions, not to shame us, but to draw us closer and remind us that His nature is steady, even when life feels unstable. She gives voice to the questions many of us have whispered in hard seasons of waiting: Lord, do you care? Have you forgotten me? Are you punishing me?

Drawing on her own experiences, she encourages us to examine the thoughts, fears, and beliefs that shape our understanding of God. She points us toward a hopeful truth: Jesus sometimes allows these painful seasons because He sees the outcome and longs to reveal more of Himself along the way.

If your waiting feels like God is withholding from you, then you will find this book both refreshing and resourceful. You'll be refreshed to know you are not alone, that others have walked through waiting and discovered beauty on the other side. And you'll find Jen's stories and biblical insights to be a valuable resource when you feel stuck, lost, or discouraged during a time of waiting.

So, read this book slowly. Let it encourage your soul. And then share it with others who are waiting, inviting them to trust God more deeply.

Introduction
Living Out of Tune

I recently attended a local high school choir concert. The evening was a medley of choral arrangements, a few well-harmonized quartets, and a smattering of solos. At one point, an enthusiastic student took the stage with a piano accompanist. The pianist launched into a peppy showtune number, and the young girl began to sing. She started off strong and then, ever so slightly, tip-toed out of key. Her note was barely discordant, but it was enough to snap the audience to attention. It was obvious something was wrong, and the audience could feel the tension.

We began to cringe.

We knew the piano's notes were right, and it was the vocalist who needed the slight adjustment. As parents, we all wanted to rescue her. In real time, we were watching her most embarrassing moment unfold. A story she would tell for years to come! Thankfully, after three minutes, the performance was over. The soloist quietly exited the stage, and the audience exhaled a collective sigh of relief.

When two notes don't harmonize, the sound is jarring and uncomfortable. Even to the untrained ear, it is clear that something is amiss. The longer the tension continues, the more desperate we are to resolve it.

And the same can be said of life.

Sometimes my circumstances don't harmonize with my expectations of God. It creates a restlessness in me that I can't resolve. I have looked at certain situations and wondered why God was not orchestrating change. To me, the fulfillment of my longings was the simple solution to the unpleasant tone ringing in my ears.

I have also experienced a desire that shouts through a megaphone in my heart and then leaves me wondering why God was silent in response to it. How can I feel so passionately about something that my Heavenly Father seems to ignore?

These experiences cause me to feel out of tune with Him and out of sync with my own heart. And it is very confusing. I am asking for good things! Why wouldn't He want this for me? I know He can answer my prayers. So why won't He?

God is the tried-and-true notes of the piano. His tunes ring out with goodness and love. My unmet desires, and the circumstances surrounding them, are like the off-key notes from the teenage vocalist. They sound sharp in contrast, refusing to symphonize with God's nature. Appearing, in fact, to contradict Him.

This lack of harmony between God's plans and my circumstances is unpleasant. The longer the wait, the more the racket remains, forcing me to listen to conflicting tones grating uncomfortably against one another. Over time, it only grows louder and more distressing.

This tension of feeling slightly off-key with God is real. Like the high school vocalist, I can slowly tiptoe out of harmony—unknowingly at first. It starts with a hope or a desire or even an idea that emerges in my heart. First it taps lightly to the beat of my existing life and then it gently increases in volume. It seems to fit so well into the musical measure God has already established. Surely it belongs! Surely my thoughts are His, and surely this is what He wants for me too.

Why wouldn't He want this relationship to be restored?

Why wouldn't He want this healing to occur?

Why wouldn't He want this career or these children I long for?

Surely these are His plans for me.

Somewhere along the way I attempt to harmonize my plans with His. I grab hold of my dreams and hopes, confident they will complement His plans. But my circumstances don't change. At first, I am resolute and remain steadfast. I long for God to work in my life in that one specific way. Over time, however, His silence quietly erodes at my heart. Why wouldn't God want this in my life? It is good, logical, and even honoring to Him.

I keep waiting.

Soon He will bring my notes into harmony with His.

Surely.

As time ticks on, I can hear the dissonance increase. And the louder it gets, the more confused I become. Tones of disappointment begin to seep in. Then frustration. What is God waiting for? It feels counterintuitive for God not to act in this area of my life. Then somewhere in that journey of waiting, I begin to wonder something. It tickles the outside edges of my mind and then slowly moves to the forefront. Doubt creeps in, and anger starts to quietly rumble deep within me.

Why is God withholding this from me?

If you are reading these words, I assume it is because you have walked, or are walking, a similar road. You have battled with uncertainty and have longed to understand God's ways. You know what it is to cry out only to find silence on the other end. You might even wish your longings would let go of the vice grip they have on your heart and let you move on.

If that is the case, I am so glad you are here.

I want to invite you to journey with me in the pages to come. I can't promise that all of your dreams will come true, that God will put an end to what grieves you, or that you will somehow speed up your season of waiting. I can, however, promise to take an honest look at waiting and address the insecurities that surface as a result.

I want to consider questions like: Does God withhold from us? If yes, then when does He do it and why? Psalm 84:11 says, "... no good thing does he withhold from those whose walk is blameless." Does this mean we are guaranteed what we want as long as we are jumping through all the right spiritual hoops? Conversely, is it because of our own mistakes or poor choices that God bridles our desires?

In Matthew 7:7-11, Jesus tells us to ask,

seek, and knock in prayer. And that, "your Father in heaven gives good gifts to those who ask him!" So, why are our prayers not being answered? How do we reconcile this passage with our current situation?

Or what about this thought: When waiting *feels* like withholding... is this just a feeling or is it really happening? How do we trust God when we doubt His goodness?

My sincere hope is that as we wrestle with these questions, we will learn to find peace in the midst of the pain and certainty in the most uncertain of situations. They are available to us! And God is faithful to provide them. We don't have to remain stuck in frustration and disappointment. God has taught me a lot and continues to teach me what to do with waiting, silence, and unmet expectations. I am still a work in progress but am looking forward to sharing the nuggets I have learned along the way and still need to revisit regularly.

Please know that nothing in this book will teach you how to twist God's arm or somehow manipulate your circumstances in your favor. Rather, these chapters will guide you to something better. Something deeper. Something actually worth the wait.

Do you feel out of tune with God in your life right now? That's ok. You can rediscover harmony with Him. I promise.

Let's get started...

*Section One:
The Weight of
the Wait*

Chapter One
The In-Between

Years ago, my family and I vacationed for a few days in Manhattan. My two sons were teenagers at the time, so it was the perfect age. They were young enough to be adventurous, yet old enough to handle lots (and lots) of walking. We stood atop Rockefeller Plaza, strolled through Central Park, and gawked at the diamonds at Tiffany's (ok, maybe that was just me). We witnessed the chaos of Grand Central Station, toured the 9/11 museum, and even got our 15 minutes of fame by jumping up and down as the cameras panned the TODAY show crowd. And, oh, the food! We ate bagels, pizza, cheesecake, and loads of other iconic NYC must-haves.

But as we toured the city, we couldn't help but notice the dirty streets, the incessant honking, and the constant pressure to move fast. At one point, utterly exhausted from our sightseeing, we hailed a cab in order to avoid walking five more city blocks to the next subway stop. The price of the cab was worth it, though it took over an hour to get through traffic!

For us, Manhattan was a great place to visit, but not a place where we would want to live.

And can't that be said of our spiritual lives, too? Aren't there places we are happy to visit, but don't want to reside there? Consider the idea of waiting.

Waiting starts off exciting. Knowing the potential that lies ahead, we brim with anticipation. We pray in faith, revel in God's power, and look forward to Him ushering in something wonderful. We naturally create scenarios with this new addition. Our hearts are hopeful!

As time stretches on, however, our fortitude begins to wane. Our faith gets a little wobbly, and we question God's ways. Often, silence becomes God's primary mode of communication, and weariness creeps into the crevices of our hearts. As anticipation morphs into disappointment, we slowly decide that waiting isn't fun anymore.

We want to visit waiting, but we don't want to live there.

Do you have a dream that tugs at your

heart? Maybe it is a relationship you long to restore? Or a healing you hope will occur? What about an idea that seems so perfectly fit for you, your personality, or your current stage in life?

Something that is yet to be fulfilled.

The place between the inception of a desire and its outcome is what I like to call the in-between. It is where we start off full of adventure and excitement but grow restless as the desire gets stronger and the wait gets longer. Add what feels like little or no response from God to the mix and you have a recipe for heartache. Over time, we find ourselves caught between two desires: a longing to fulfill our dreams or the hope that they will be so far removed from our hearts that we can move on contentedly without them.

But please, God, don't leave me in the in-between.

The in-between is a tricky place to navigate because uncertainty can be found around almost any corner. Not knowing the outcome slowly chips away at our peace and our patience, and eventually our faith. If we knew our desires would be guaranteed, we could wait as long as necessary to achieve them. Likewise, if we knew they would never happen, we could grieve appropriately and move on. But don't say, "maybe." Uncertainty simultaneously produces both the anticipation that it could happen and the disappointment that it hasn't.

The in-between is hard.

It is a place devoid of our control. We can say we trust God, but in this place, we have no other option. There is no way to manipulate or manufacture our circumstances, so all we can do is look to Him. Our backs are pinned against the wall with no place to turn. And oh, the aches and pains of that position!

And dare I mention the silence? What about the long stretches of straining to hear His voice? The passage of time where the conversation feels terribly one-sided. The confusion increases as the level of communication decreases. Oh, how I have experienced this and will share some of my stories later in the book. Silence is so hard, and I have learned that silence is often the main thoroughfare through the in-between.

Sigh.

As much as we would like to avoid this undesired journey, as followers of Christ we will all spend time in the in-between. The Israelites spent 40 years wandering in the desert. And then another 70 in Babylonian exile. Abraham and Sarah waited a long time to get pregnant, and so did Hannah. Noah set sail for an undetermined amount of time and remained in that boat for over 200 days *after* the 40 consecutive nights of rain. And don't forget the time between the last words in the Old Testament and the birth of Jesus—that was over 400 years. The in-between was not unfamiliar territory for our scriptural sojourners, and it is not unfamiliar to us today. Here is the bottom line:

If you plan to walk with Jesus, you can expect some time in the in-between.

God has been and will continue to use waiting in our lives. This is an intentional choice He makes, knowing it will teach us lessons we would never have learned otherwise, shape us in ways we didn't know we needed, and grow us further than we thought we were capable of.

Waiting is not a mistake.

It doesn't occur because God is unorganized or indecisive. He is not overwhelmed nor confused. Rather, it is a tool He has been using with mankind from the beginning, knowing it leads us to depend on Him.

So if we can count on this being part of our journey, can we learn to do it well? Is it possible to find a way to accept it and learn from it versus hating it and trying not to drown in it?

Is it possible to have hope in the waiting? What about peace? Or even joy?

Some of our greatest barriers to hope, peace, and joy in the in-between are the questions that lurk within that space. Questions we like to keep at bay because they make us shift uncomfortably in our spiritual seats. They rattle our faith and unearth emotions we would rather keep as vocabulary words instead of sentiments we actually feel. Questions like these:

God, do you care about me?

Have you forgotten me?

Are you punishing me?

Do you still love me?

You might be afraid to ask those questions out loud. I know I've asked them in the quiet places of my heart, hoping God didn't actually hear them. Can I ask these questions and still have faith? It felt wrong to ask them, and what if I didn't like the answer? Where would my faith be if I determined God was not as good as I had always thought He was?

If you find yourself in the in-between, I am guessing there are some questions hiding just below the surface. And that's ok. God is not afraid of your questions. Or mine. In fact, He welcomes them. And strangely enough, He knows that deep down we are all asking the same tiny question. Though our in-betweens might look vastly different, we are all struggling with the same small three-letter query:

Why?

Now, don't get me wrong. This tiny question will not have a tiny answer. It may be small in stature, but it is incredibly dense and weighty.

God, why are you allowing this? Not preventing this? Not fixing this? Not providing this? Not _____?

Why, God? I am so confused.

And sad.

And angry.

And disappointed.

That tiny question is laden with emotion. And if we aren't careful, those emotions can begin to drown out our faith.

It is critical that we understand God's character before we enter the in-between. Do we see Him as a policeman or a judge? As a soft-hearted parent or a distant, impersonal one? Hard times often reveal our assumptions about Him. Therefore, it is so important our understanding of His character is accurate.

And based on experience.

We can't rely on surface Sunday School descriptions of Him. Rather, we need the truth of His nature to trickle down into how we experience Him. Knowledge is not enough. His character must be anchored in our hearts. Why? Because He doesn't change. He is the same in every situation

(Hebrews 13:8). And during seasons of uncertainty, we need to count on the fact that He is consistent, unwavering, and trustworthy.

The questions that surface in the in-between are simply our contradictions of His nature. They are the doubts that creep up when suddenly our circumstances don't match our expectations of Him. Therefore, it is imperative that we know Him before we face a season of waiting. Otherwise, we might find ourselves in one of the following scenarios:

If God cares about me, then won't He notice when I'm hurting? As the pain mounts without any reprieve, I fear I am invisible to Him.

God, do you still care about me?

When more time passes than I am comfortable with, I wonder if God still knows the number of hairs on my head. Does He still see me? Am I still His beloved child?

God, have you forgotten me?

When the pain becomes unbearable, my thoughts race for an explanation. Though God forgives and does not keep a record of wrongs, I can't help but entertain the idea that some horrible mistake is hanging over me.

God, are you punishing me?

And when I plead with God for a desire that aches within me, I don't know why He would withhold it from me. What about the abundant life? And the good gifts He gives His children?

God, do you still love me?

God is not afraid of our questions because He knows the emotions that lurk behind them, as well as the danger they can cause. He welcomes our questions so He can protect us from using them to define who we think He should be. Let me explain.

It is easy to slip into the place where our pain reshapes our understanding of God. We choose to define (or redefine) the attributes of God based on our situation. We give our emotions more authority than they deserve. When we allow our expectations, assumptions, and actual circumstances to cloud our understanding of who He is, we only further cloud our experience in the in-between.

Take God's goodness, for example.

A painful period of waiting, without relief or resolution, can create mounds of disappointment and anger. And those emotions can then rewrite the script to say God's goodness is something that comes and goes. It is dependent on something we do or don't do. It fluctuates depending on how God feels that day or how well we behave.

And therein lies the danger: if we choose to define God's goodness based on our own assumptions and expectations, then anything contradictory will cause us not to question goodness in general, but to question Him.

God's nature does not change, but sometimes goodness won't be wrapped in the package we think it should.

For years after my second son was born, I struggled with chronic back pain. I learned that pregnancy naturally relaxes the muscles around the abdomen and back and that some women's muscles never "bounce back." During that season, I regularly injured myself. And it was always doing something ridiculously commonplace like getting out of the car or reaching over the bed to grab a blanket. But it would take me down in an instant. And then I would spend the next 7-10 days visiting the chiropractor and resting on the couch.

Mornings were also especially challenging at that time. Gone were the days when I could jump out of bed and immediately hit the ground running. Now I had to start slowly. Very slowly. I would get up, slip into my house shoes, make some tea, and sit on the couch. I needed a good hour to warm up before I could really get moving.

At first, it was frustrating. I am Type A through and through and never face the day without a to-do list in hand. But the pain was real, and the fear of exacerbating it by leaping into the day prematurely was real too. I complied. I started my day by sitting.

Now, if I am going to sit for an hour every morning, I might as well read my Bible, right? Prior to this season, I did make time to read, but it was definitely a shorter amount of time, and it wasn't every single day. But now my body was forcing me to be still. And what I discovered was how much I had been missing out.

Due to this new routine, I was able to read more, but I was also able to linger more. I could mull over a certain verse. Ponder how something applied to my life. I had more time to journal. I had more time to pray. And as my kids grew to be toddlers, and later preschoolers, they learned to crawl out of bed and onto the same couch with me. They would quietly climb up and put their heads on my lap or on my shoulder, waiting for me to finish. Such sweet bliss! I cherished it every morning knowing one day they would outgrow the ritual.

After several years of starting my day this way out of physical necessity, I grew to do so out of personal necessity. I learned to love it. To want it. To need it. What started out as hard and frustrating, slowly transformed into something beautiful. Something lasting.

My sweet connection with God was wrapped

in the goodness of back pain. At first I didn't like it, but now I can see how God used a hard thing to forge a good thing into my heart.

Have you ever had a challenging experience that produced something positive in your life? Can you reflect in hindsight and see God's hand in it? You might have doubted His goodness at certain points along the way, but in the end, can you see His love in it? He *knew* what it would produce in you. He saw the end result and pressed on to get you there.

We can't let our pain reshape our understanding of God. Trusting that God is all-knowing, all-powerful, and ever-present is crucial to our ability to navigate the in-between. We must stand on the fact that He knows it all, our past, present, and future, and how it fits together. And we don't need to be afraid of the questions that will surface. Rather, we can use them to uncover whatever aspect of God's character we might be doubting—simply because we don't like our circumstances.

So where do we begin? *Oh, to snap our* fingers and suddenly see our season of waiting as a glorious expression of God's love and care! If only it were that simple. Instead, we need to revisit our basic understanding of God. There's a critical piece we must nail down if we want to navigate the in-between. Without this, our emotions will always be quick to write and rewrite our expectations of God. But we will get to that in the next chapter.

For now, let's end with a deep breath. Not happy in the in-between? That's ok. I doubt any of us will ever grow to love waiting, but I am confident we can shift our perspective enough that the weight of emotion shifts too.

Sit for a minute with these statements. Read them slowly, one at a time, and let them sink in. If you struggle to believe any of them, ask God to make them clear to you in the pages to come and in the depths of your heart. Then, close with the truth of God's character found in Scripture.

God cares about me.

I am not forgotten.

He is not punishing me.

He loves me.

> He is the "...Father of the heavenly lights, who does not change like shifting shadows"
> James 1:17
>
> "For I the Lord do not change; therefore you, O children of Jacob, are not consumed"
> Malachi 3:6
>
> "Jesus Christ is the same yesterday and today and forever"
> Hebrews 13:8

Chapter Two
The Partnership

"Black Magic, Witchcraft and the Occult"

That was the title of the speech I critiqued my freshman year in college. My friend, Christie and I were taking a public speaking course and one of our assignments was to attend any lecture on campus and write a report on how well it was delivered. After scanning the activity board at the student center, our curiosity was piqued by this simple flyer. It promised to be interesting.

That evening, a wide variety of students were milling about, ranging from those who clearly dabbled in the dark side to those who were just plain curious. Christie and I, notebooks in hand, took a seat.

The speaker walked on stage in khakis and

a button down and I remember thinking he was not what I was expecting. He began his speech with a very clear thesis:

"I am a Christian, and I am here to speak against black magic, witchcraft, and the occult."

There was an audible groan in the room. It was a classic case of bait and switch! Christie and I exchanged glances, knowing the interest level in the speech had now dramatically dropped. Nonetheless, we needed the credit, so we poised our pens and waited for more.

I honestly don't remember much of what the guy said. He began spouting off Bible verses fairly quickly, so I was lost from the start. At one point I leaned over and asked my friend if she understood his biblical references. Her response was straightforward, "No."

A student seated in front of us overheard our brief exchange, turned around in his seat, and offered to further explain the speaker's message. We shrugged and nodded apathetically. The guy quickly whipped out a tiny booklet that explained how to become a Christian. He proceeded to walk us through each page. It was brand new information to me. I found out later it was called a gospel tract, but at the time I was clueless.

I had heard about Jesus dying on the cross, but I had never thought of it on a personal level. I knew what sin meant, but I had never thought of myself as a sinner. Every page of the tract intrigued me. I had made mistakes in life. I did want to get rid of them. I *longed* for a fresh start. Though I had never heard the gospel message before, it completely resonated in my heart.

I looked at Christie and could tell she felt the same way. We were experiencing something reverent and were unsure how to respond. Suddenly overwhelmed with emotion, we both began to cry. To say that our front-seat neighbor was surprised is an understatement.

Immediately, we began to press him for more information. We wanted to be forgiven and grab hold of this gift of eternal life but had no idea how. The verbiage was foreign to us, but we got the concept, and were all in. We asked him what to do next. He paused, pointed to a written prayer on the back of the tract and said, "Why don't you pray this out loud?"

So, that's what we did.

Right there in that auditorium.

Students were chatting and starting to file out, and Christie and I were crying and praying out loud with a total stranger.

I came home that night after not learning about black magic and couldn't sleep. I was so excited! The problem was I didn't know what to do next. I didn't own a Bible, didn't go to church, and didn't know anyone who did. All I had was the little booklet that explained the gospel. I noticed the name of a student ministry on the back of it and discovered they had a weekly meeting. So, later that week, I went.

I remember standing outside a room full of loud music, loads of Mexican food, and students laughing and hanging out. It looked so fun, but my feet felt frozen to the floor. I waited, wanting to enter, but feeling so out of place. People were coming and going all around me, but no one said hello. I was scanning for the guy who had given me the gospel tract but couldn't find him. I still didn't fully understand the decision I had made, so I was uncomfortable entering. What if someone asked me why I was there?

After a few awkward minutes, I left. And I never tried to go again.

Which leads to the second half of my story:

Fast forward six months. I was a sophomore and had made the decision to transfer to a college two states away. I didn't know a soul but was ready for a new adventure. I packed up and moved into the dorm.

Though I was in a brand-new place, I was continually reminded of my experience with Christie. Something had happened to me that night, and I couldn't shake it. Even months later! I finally pulled out my student handbook (pre-internet days) and looked up religion. I searched and found the one I recognized.

I dialed the number and Ronnie, the campus minister, answered. I explained that someone had given me a little booklet, and I had prayed the prayer on the back. Then, I cut to the chase and asked the question that had been burning in my heart for months:

"Do I just go to heaven when I die, or is there more to experience here in this life?"

Ronnie wisely suggested I come to his office and let him answer that in person.

I hung up, laced up my shoes, and marched over to his office. It was there that he expounded on what the tract had left out. He put me in a Bible study and introduced me to a few girls who would later show me how to pray, understand Scripture, and wrestle with my faith.

Fast forward almost 30 years, and my faith journey has defined my life. I have watched God become real and relevant right before my eyes. I have witnessed answered prayers in ways I cannot explain. I have come to Him in need and marveled at His creative provision in return. I have been broken, stuck, and scared and amazed at how the Bible spoke to my issues and guided me out of them. I have watched my life unfold with purpose and meaning, and I'm grateful for the plans He has for me.

As you can see, my story is divided into two sections. My freshman year of college, I learned about Jesus. My sophomore year and beyond, I partnered with Jesus. Clearly, both involve Jesus, but in different ways. And this difference is what we need when navigating a season of waiting.

Now, it is so easy to want to jump to the next section of this book and dive into the painful questions we want answered. But unless we have a clear understanding of how to partner with Jesus, we will continue to struggle. A partnership is crucial if we want to navigate our seasons of waiting with peace, hope, and even joy.

And a partnership is different from a relationship.

You may have heard Christianity defined as a relationship and not a religion. Meaning, our faith is not defined by a checklist of things to do, rather a personal bond you maintain with Jesus Christ. I do agree with that distinction, but I would argue the word relationship doesn't accurately describe it, either.

Consider the way God spoke to Abraham, revealing the fact that he would soon become the father of a great nation, the Israelites, God's chosen people (Genesis 12:1-3). What a privilege! And what about Moses? The man God selected to rescue His people from enslavement in Egypt (Exodus 3:1-10). Or Daniel, who faced the lion's den because he disregarded the king's mandate and would not stop praying (Daniel 6:10). And don't forget the disciples who left everything to travel with Jesus, learn from Jesus, tell people about Jesus, and later (most of them) die for Jesus.

These people had something deeper than just a relationship with God. He interacted with them and revealed His plans to them. He invited them into His greater purposes and proved Himself faithful, powerful, and worthy. And it wasn't always easy for them! He called them to do things beyond their comfort zone and stretched them in ways that taught them how to depend on Him. He did things through them they could not have done on their own.

No, God wants more than a relationship with us.

He wants a partnership.

A partnership differs from a relationship because a relationship has the potential to be optional. Have you ever moved away and simply lost touch with someone? Have you known someone who chose a different path in life, had a bunch of kids, or a demanding career and you grew apart? Have you ever liked someone until, well… until you didn't? Relationships come and go for lots of different reasons. And a relationship with Jesus is no different. People come and go with Him too.

Especially in the in-between.

Sometimes a painful season of waiting will bring you straight into a relationship with Jesus. You are desperate, overwhelmed, and aware that you need something bigger than yourself. So, you run to Him, plead, and pour out your heart. You scour the Scriptures looking for Him. It's personal.

But the opposite can also be said. Sometimes the in-between causes people to walk away from a relationship with Jesus. They cannot reconcile their circumstances with His character and choose to sever any and all interaction with Him. It's also personal—but in a different way.

Relationships are optional. That is why Jesus wants more than a relationship with you. He never wants to be optional in your life because you are not—and never will be—optional to Him.

A partnership is different from a relationship because of its unwavering commitment. But that is not the only difference. What also sets it apart is the fact that there is a plan involved. A greater purpose in mind. A mission. A goal. And together, the participants within that partnership work to achieve that predetermined goal.

But therein lies the rub.

When you are in a partnership with God, He gets to pick the goal.

And that fact can quickly become a point of contention during the tenure of an in-between. The common denominator between anyone waiting for *anything* is this: we know what we want. We have our own goals.

This is the point when people who are not Christians take offense. And I don't blame them. On paper, it can look cruel or even tyrannical. Why does God get to call all the shots, and we have to willingly submit? Even as believers this is a continual struggle. It is human nature to want our way. It is hard to relinquish your own goals and adopt His. Especially when His goal seems so self-centered.

So what is the goal?

God's number one priority in life is to make Himself known to the world. This has always been His objective. Consider the Israelites. Why did God create the Jewish nation of Israel?

"And who is like your people Israel—the one nation on earth that God went out to redeem as a people for himself, and to *make a name for himself,* and to perform great and awesome wonders by driving out nations and their gods from before your people, whom you redeemed from Egypt?" (2 Samuel 7:23, emphasis mine)

The Jews were God's chosen people not

because He liked them better but because He had chosen them to make a name for Himself. So why make His name great?

God doesn't strive for this because He is egotistical or narcissistic. Rather, in pointing to Himself, He illuminates the path away from sin. This was what first drew me to God when I was a freshman in college. When I read that gospel tract, no one had to convince me that I had made mistakes. I didn't need anyone to explain to me the woes of guilt, regret, or shame. Though I had never referred to myself as a sinner before, I very much knew I was one. But as quickly as I learned I was a sinner, I turned the page and learned I could be forgiven. I could let go of those burdens and start fresh again. How amazing!

God is on a mission. He knows our sin not only separates us from Him, but it shackles us and chips away at all the good He has prepared for us. Sin is not for us; it is against us. And God loves us so much that He wants to open our eyes to the state of our sin and our absolute need for Him.

God makes Himself known to rescue us from the sin that is destroying us.

If you think that sounds too dramatic, consider the words of the prophet Jeremiah, "The heart is deceitful above all things and beyond cure. Who can understand it?" (Jeremiah 17:9)

We cannot comprehend the depth of our deceit. And we are beyond cure. We are fooling ourselves if we think otherwise! If it were up to us, we would set out to make ourselves known. We already make ourselves the center of our own universe, right? Consider how you map out your day every morning. Don't you arrange everything you do around what you need and what you want? How often do you tweak things in your day simply because it serves you better? Have you ever cut a slice of cake for someone and made sure yours was just a tiny bit bigger?

You get my point.

So how does this affect our seasons of waiting? Consider these questions: How do we know what we long for is best for us? Even as good and godly and wonderful as that "thing" is, might there be a chance it's not as good and godly and wonderful as we think?

Our hearts are deceitful, no matter how hard we argue otherwise. So, yes, people take offense at the thought of God governing their lives, but the alternative is scarier in my opinion. I don't want to be in charge of everything in my life. Why would I trust my deceitful heart and limited understanding when I have access to someone with a pure heart and unlimited understanding?

God makes Himself known to rescue us from ourselves.

He does this by inviting us into a partnership with Him. It is within the bounds of that connection with Him we are safe.

But, boy, can that be hard sometimes.

Let's see how Jesus did this and what we can learn from Him.

The story opens in John 11 with Mary and Martha sending word to Jesus that their brother Lazarus is ill. They want Him to come and heal him. But Jesus stays put for three days, and Lazarus dies. The story is hard to read because not only did Jesus not come, but He chose not to come.

Until later.

In their hearts and later with their words, both sisters cried out, "Lord, if you had been here, my brother would not have died!" (John 11:21,32) Translation (cue the tiny question from chapter 1): *Why,* Jesus? Why didn't you come and heal our brother?"

But lo and behold, Jesus had an answer for them! And His answer came in the form of a prayer. He stood outside the tomb and cried out to God.

"Father, I thank you that you have heard me. I knew that you always hear me, but I said this for the benefit of the people standing here, that they may believe that you sent me. When he had said this, Jesus called in a loud voice, 'Lazarus, come out!'" (John 11:41-43).

And then Lazarus appeared at the entrance of the tomb, wrapped in a burial cloth, but very much alive.

Jesus allowed Lazarus to die and put Mary and Martha through a torturous in-between so that the people in that town (and later so many more people!) would believe that God sent Jesus to earth. He knew the grief it would cause the siblings, but He also knew the impact Lazarus' resurrected life would make. Mary and Martha wanted a healing, but Jesus wanted a resurrection. And He knew the joy that would result from such a miraculous moment. In short, the waiting Mary and Martha (and Lazarus) endured was part of a much bigger story.

Because Jesus knew the ending, He initiated the in-between.

Please don't rush past that last sentence. It's packed with so much truth.

Jesus knows our past, present, and future. He is never frightened, forgetful, or frazzled, and nothing takes Him by surprise. His actions are always deliberate decisions aimed at reaching His intended goal: making God known to others.

Also, Jesus knew their grief would not compare to the miracle they would soon witness. He was not swayed by hard situations because He knew joy was right around the corner. He also knew this scenario would draw out everyone's weaknesses. It was going to be more than they could handle, causing them to lean into Him, which would lead them to discover more of Him.

Please note there are some aspects of God that we can only experience through difficultly. He doesn't want us to know Him superficially. He wants to reveal the deep layers of His presence in our lives, and that requires some digging. Some unearthing of ourselves. Some undoing of our self-sufficiency. Jesus is okay with the in-between because He knows what it will reveal and produce—in ourselves and Him. All good things.

Therefore, when it comes to waiting, we have to trust that the impetus behind God's actions is love. We see this love clearly in verses 5-6: "Now Jesus loved Martha and her sister and Lazarus. So when he heard that Lazarus was sick, he stayed where he was two more days..." Because Jesus loved them, He didn't rush to them. So counterintuitive! He let Lazarus die so they would not only receive more than they could imagine, but they would witness God making His name great.

This is why a partnership is so critical. Sometimes our circumstances look as bleak as they did the day Lazarus died. We need a reason to trust God's love for us in those moments. We need to know God still has us in His hands.

Without a partnership, you will continually be in danger of defining or redefining your understanding of God based on your circumstances. You will fall prey to wanting your plan so much that you lose sight of His. Your tunnel vision will prevent the proper perspective: that your story is a part of a bigger story.

God's plans might hurt at times. Mary and Martha were devastated when Lazarus died. But they didn't see the full picture until later. They didn't know a resurrection was on the way. So just as we know God never stopped loving Mary and Martha, we can trust He will never stop loving us either. Our waiting is not an indication that God is cruel. It is simply an indication that He is doing something we can't see yet.

A partnership is what maintains that perspective.

Not every situation will have a quick and radical bow on top like Mary and Martha experienced. Sometimes our waiting stretches on for months, years or even a lifetime. In Hebrews we read of those who didn't get a "happy ending."

"These were all commended for their faith, yet none of them received what had been promised, since God had planned something better for us so that only together with us would they be made perfect" (Hebrews 11:39-40).

When Waiting Feels Like Withholding

God sees beyond your lifetime. People like Abraham, Isaac, Jacob, and Sarah partnered with God, adopted His plan, and set their trajectory in that direction. They did their best to keep the goal at the forefront of their minds as they endured challenging, and sometimes violent, twists and turns in life. They got sidetracked along the way (more than once), but they were still known for "living by faith." They welcomed their promises from a distance.

God's plan included more than them in order to be fulfilled. There was a bigger story. A larger plan. A greater purpose. And it involved more people and more generations.

As we wait on Him, we have to remind ourselves to maintain that perspective. And remember this is a partnership based on trust.

Much like Abraham, we may not see the full fruition of God's specific work—we are not guaranteed a bow on top of every situation. What is guaranteed, however, is God's commitment to us. His faithfulness to us. I take great comfort in that. Because if there is even the slightest chance that God could grow fickle, indecisive, or weak, I know that seed of doubt would creep in and take root. But no. His partnership with us is sure.

Solid.

Trustworthy.

We are not optional to Him.

So, the question is, have you partnered with Him? Or is He just a religion or a relationship to you?

I recognize that a partnership with God isn't always easy. In several seasons of my life, I desperately searched for answers to my "why" questions. I struggled to trust Him when I had conflicting emotions directed toward Him. I didn't know how to hold both trust and disappointment at the same time. Could anger and faith co-exist? Could I overcome confusion without clear answers?

In the next section, we are going to look at some commonly asked questions that lurk in the shadows of the in-between. The topics and questions we often wonder about and wrestle with but are nervous to explore. What will happen to our faith if we boldly ask these tough questions? What if God doesn't have an answer or we don't like the answer? Together we will explore these topics and what Scripture has to say about them.

But for now, I want you to consider this partnership. Do you need to begin one? If you have never established a relationship with Jesus, start there. Admit you are a sinner, receive His forgiveness, and commit to partnering with Him from this day forward. Maybe you simply need to recommit to your partnership and reacquaint yourself with His mission and focus on trusting. As this chapter closes, spend some time evaluating what is in your heart.

I want to leave you with a beautiful picture of what a partnership with God looks like. It is an old hymn that is still sung to this day. It perfectly describes the trust that is needed, but more than that, it describes what happens when we are able to trust. I will let the words speak for themselves:

When peace like a river attendeth my way,

When sorrows like sea billows roll;

Whatever my lot Thou hast taught me to say,

"It is well, it is well with my soul!"

It can be well with our souls. When we are in the midst of peace or in the throes of sorrow, we can say, "It is well, it is well with my soul."

You may not feel that way right now, nor can you imagine ever feeling that way. That's ok. But please know that is where we are headed. Join me as we learn to trust more, fear less. As we learn to lay down our expectations and embrace His.

It is possible to be well with our souls, even in the midst of waiting.

Let's close in prayer. If now is not a good time, make a note to do this later. Otherwise, take a moment to sit quietly and slow yourself down. Put your to-do list aside and turn your phone off. Take a few minutes to talk to God about your situation. Tell Him what scares you, what you don't understand, and any emotions you feel. Consider the following prayer:

Lord, waiting is hard. The unknown is even harder. You know my emotions and how I feel about my season of waiting. But today I acknowledge that you are in control of my situation. There is no detail that escapes you or takes you by surprise. Will you help me to trust you today? Give me faith to believe there is a purpose in this. Help me reconcile my conflicting emotions. Strengthen my partnership with you and help my heart to make your plans my plans as well. Do in me what I cannot do myself. Help me to say it is well with my soul. In Jesus' name, Amen.

*Section Two:
The Answers
We Seek*

Chapter Three
Lord, Don't You Care?

I have two sons, and they both have great hair. Though one has more wavy locks, they both have thick, envious curls. When my older son was a junior in high school, he grew it out a bit on top and had a fantastic mess of well-defined curls. No frizz or frazzle. It was a good look that looked good on him.

The week before his senior year began, however, he got a haircut. I will never forget the expression on his face when he returned home. He had asked for less than an inch off but left the building with at least three gone. And considering he only had 4 or so inches to start with, that left him a tad shy of scalped.

It was brutal.

School was starting in a week, yearbook pictures were in two weeks, and the senior beach retreat was in three. All big milestones that would now be memorialized with a borderline buzz cut. It was a dark day in our household as we all tried to console him and tell him, "It didn't look that bad."

He asked me if there was anything he could do. Was there a special shampoo, cream, or pill he could take to grow his hair back faster? Like any good mom I at least Googled the idea. But I knew deep down I wouldn't find anything other than gimmicks. The only thing he could do was wait for it to grow back out.

I felt his angst.

Many years ago, the week before I started graduate school, I, too, experienced a haircut disaster. During orientation, I saw a girl walk across campus with an adorable pixie cut. It was cut short in the back and on the sides with a stylish wind-blown look on top. What I didn't take into consideration was the fact that she had thick, barely wavy hair. And I have thin, ultrafine curly hair. And I had just moved to a state with considerable humidity and didn't know the havoc that it would wreak on my fragile locks. I have never been known for fashion or beauty (or weather) expertise, and this lack of knowledge cost me considerably.

I came out of the salon all frizz and frazzle. Picture light, airy, terribly thin hair, wafting in the wind. In time, I slowly morphed into a light brown version of Toad on Mario Cart. I went through a headband stage, a barrette stage, and a variety of bobby pin stages until, after about 10 months, I had a decent hairstyle again.

It was brutal.

So, when my son came home with the worst haircut of his life, it broke my heart. His eyes said it all. *Help me. Please!* And I wanted to! I deeply cared, and he knew it. I would have done anything to will his hair to grow faster, but all I could do was hug him and tell him I was so sorry.

And to never go back to that place again.

When we are in desperate situations, it is easy to plead with God. To look at Him with frantic eyes, begging Him to do something. And when we don't hear anything or see change, we can't help but ask, "Lord, don't you care?"

In Mark 4, the disciples asked Jesus that very question. The scene took place by a lake. Jesus had been teaching at the shore all day, and a significantly sized crowd had formed. As the end of the day drew near, Jesus suggested they travel to the other side of the lake. It was a simple suggestion and one the disciples had done many times before. Transportation by boat was normal.

So, they piled in, pushed off, and began the trek. Without warning, though, a storm swept over them. The waves were crashing, and the boat was rapidly filling up. The disciples were terrified. And what was Jesus doing?

Sleeping on a cushion in the back.

Frantic, the disciples woke Him. They cried out to Him with fervor. The question at the forefront of their minds, and of utmost priority, came tumbling out of them.

"Don't you care if we drown?" (v. 38)

They were astonished that Jesus was sleeping. An emergency was unfolding all around them, and He was taking a nap? It was unthinkable. What was wrong with Him?

Don't. You. Care.

Those three words are heavy with emotion. For the disciples, their question communicated their greatest fears and doubts. They were overwhelmed. They had no viable solutions and felt there wasn't time left to find one. And Jesus' sleepy state led them to one conclusion: He didn't care. Because if He did, He wouldn't be lounging on a cushion.

But *did* Jesus care?

Yes, absolutely. He just wasn't concerned about the same things they were.

Between thunder claps the disciples cried out, and the response was immediate.

Jesus wiped the cobwebs from His eyes and then commanded the wind and waves to settle down. And they did. Instantly. Easy peasy. That was that. But after the violent storm came to a stunning halt, Jesus turned to them and asked them, "Why are you so afraid? Do you still have no faith?" (v.40)

Translation: What is the big deal? Why are you freaking out?

We might be tempted to read Jesus' questions through a lens of shame. Like it was silly and ridiculous for them to get so worked up over the fact that the boat was rapidly sinking. It's just water, right? Calm down. Good grief.

But Jesus' questions weren't meant to embarrass the disciples. Rather, He was putting His finger on something deeper. Not content to let them continue living from a shallow faith, Jesus was essentially asking, "Why are you worried about *anything?* Don't you know I am bigger than any storm that could ever come your way?" This incident had revealed their hearts—the disciples had more faith in the storm than they did in Him.

The disciples took one look at the storm and had complete faith that it would destroy them. They had full confidence that this bad scenario would end catastrophically. They believed this storm would undo them. Their faith in the storm was rock solid.

It sounds funny to have faith in our circumstances, but it's certainly possible, right? Anytime we allow our situation to speak louder and have greater prominence in our minds than God, we have put our faith in it. And that is what the disciples did. They trusted in the power of the storm.

But not Jesus. He knew He was bigger than the storm. And that knowledge allowed Him to rest. Literally! He was able to lie down and sleep.

Is your faith in your circumstances? Are your fears or longings louder and more convincing than Jesus? Are you convinced the issue you are facing will completely undo you? Or do you look at the storm and know, really know, that you can still rest in the midst of it? The water might rise, and the wind might whip, but nothing, absolutely nothing, can stand against your God.

So, yes, Jesus cared. He cared about their faith. But Jesus wanted them to have faith in Him. Not the storm.

And that is not the only thing He cared about.

After Jesus quickly stilled the storm, the disciples were in shock. They were not expecting that to happen. The gospel of Mark records their response:

"They were terrified and asked each other, "Who is this? Even the wind and the waves obey him!" (Mark 4:41) Matthew's version describes them as being "amazed" (Matthew 8:27).

Bringing the storm to a screeching halt did not go unnoticed. But there was more than just miraculous weather skills at play. Jesus was up to something else: making God known.

The goal we talked about in the last chapter is back. Jesus wanted the disciples to know Him. Really understand Him. He wanted them to experience His power so they would not mistake His presence. He wanted to set Himself so far apart from the storm that there was no confusion over who was stronger.

So, again, Jesus did care. He cared that they knew He was God.

The disciples had their priorities mixed up. The goal was never to safely glide from one end of the lake to the other. The goal was to give these men a glimpse of His majesty.

And the same goes for us today.

We prefer scenic boat rides in life. We want our days to float smoothly from one to the next. We might tolerate a few waves, but no storms. Yet it is through thunder and lightning that we not only discover our weaknesses, but we discover His strength. It is through rising water and whipping wind that His holiness is revealed, and our faith is determined. Storms shake us down to what we really believe and stand for.

Jesus knows our lives are but a breath here on earth. He is aware that the boat ride of life is not very long at all. And what do we do when we reach the other side of the lake? Where will we go then? God wants to make Himself known so that when the boat ride is over, we can exit and enter into His arms for eternity.

God uses storms to help us see that He is greater than them and it strengthens our partnership with Him every time we see this greatness first hand. We can't just read that God is greater, though. We need to experience it. How can we fully appreciate His peace if we know nothing about turbulence? We don't have to like the storm. But what if we used the storm to help us see more of Him?

You might be thinking I have forgotten we are in the in-between. The place where we are waiting and not hearing much from God. The place where the storm is brewing, and Jesus is asleep. Those moments right before the disciples woke Him up were harrowing. Their faith was in the storm. The majesty of God had not shown up yet. What do we do in those moments?

I would suggest following in the footsteps of the disciples and taking the honesty route. They abruptly woke Him up and put their emotions on the line. We are scared! We are overwhelmed! We don't know what to do! Why aren't You helping us?

God is not afraid of our honesty.

So let me ask you a question. Have you ever wondered if God cares about your situation? Or have you already made the assumption that He doesn't? If so, what would you say to Him right now if you were brutally honest? Keep in mind that underneath an assumption lies the vulnerable parts that we usually try to keep hidden. By assuming He does not care, we shed light on what we are *really* feeling. In light of that:

Are you scared?

Confused?

Aching for a longing to be fulfilled?

Are you disappointed?

Angry?

Desperate for a solution of some kind?

Try articulating those feelings to Him. Put it all out there and hold nothing back. And if you have never put words to your situation and are not sure how you feel about it, sit for a minute and allow your emotions to rise to the surface. Use the following exercise to help with this conversation with Him.

Read Psalm 139:1-6. Slowly. Let each line sink in. Note how well God knows you. There is no need to hide or pretend. He knows you better than you know yourself. As you read, express whatever thoughts and feelings arise.

"You have searched me, Lord, and you know me.

You know when I sit and when I rise; you perceive my thoughts from afar.

You discern my going out and my lying down; you are familiar with all my ways.

Before a word is on my tongue, You, Lord, know it completely.

You hem me in behind and before, and you lay your hand upon me.

Such knowledge is too wonderful for me, too lofty for me to attain."

It is important to clearly understand your own thoughts and emotions about your situation. Once you have poured your heart out to Him, sit back and wait. Imagine Jesus looking into your eyes, comprehending everything you just shared, and taking your hands in His. And then listen to the questions He wants to ask you:

Do you know I am bigger than this storm? That it cannot even be compared to me? I hear your heart and know you are struggling, but will you trust me with this? If it feels too big to trust me, tell me so. Let me help you put your faith in me.

Can you see how I have been at work in your

life through this situation? If not, ask me to show you. Ask me to give you eyes to see and ears to hear and a mind to understand what I have been doing in you. Ask me to make myself known to you.

Consider grabbing a journal, opening a note on your phone, or even using the margins of this page to record your answers to these questions. Allow Psalm 139:1-6 to ground your interaction with Him and strengthen your partnership with Him. Here are some other verses you can dwell on as you commune with Him: Psalm 139:16, Proverbs 3:5-6, Jeremiah 29:13, and Mark 9:24. Put to words any experience you had with His presence. Don't rush through this.

The bottom line is yes, God does care. Sometimes, though, we need to become quiet before the Lord to recognize it. It is okay if you do not understand why you are in this waiting period. We will tackle that uncertainty in the next chapter. But for now, sit with your feelings, consider journaling your responses, and give God some time and space to speak to you.

He cares. And He wants you to know that.

Chapter Four

Can You Help Me Understand?

My younger son was diagnosed with a severe tree nut allergy at the age of two. My husband and I were shocked! There were no food allergies in our family, much less one that required us to carry an EpiPen at all times and read labels to confirm that nothing was made in a nut facility. The allergist took pains to ensure we understood the severity of his situation and shattered any hope that he would ever outgrow it.

We took inventory in our home, learned to read labels accurately, and only went to restaurants with managers who actually knew what a tree nut was. (You would be surprised!) The precautions were necessary because the allergy was real. When Parker was four, we experienced this firsthand.

We had a pecan tree in our backyard that had produced an unusually abundant harvest that winter. Even the squirrels could not keep up! We had the bright idea of bagging the nuts, wrapping them with a bow, and offering them as Christmas gifts. After growing weary of bending down to gather them, I offered to pay my older son 25 cents a bag to fill up our grocery sacks. Parker, never wanting his brother to have an edge in life, quickly wanted in on the financial endeavor. I was leery. Would it be harmful for him to touch nuts? I agreed to the business deal, with a caveat. He had to wear mittens. He happily agreed and bounced out the backdoor with dollar signs (more accurately cent signs) dancing in his head.

About ten minutes later, he came back crying, with his hands forcefully extended out in front of him. I gently pulled off the mittens only to discover his fingers were fire-engine red and had grown to the size of ballpark franks! The pecan residue had seeped through the mittens and caused his hands to react with a vengeance. I plunged his swollen appendages into bowls of ice water and administered Benadryl around the clock for two days.

Lesson learned.

That experience only heightened my fear of him swallowing a nut and made me want to always dine in the safety of our home. However, I still wanted him to enjoy outings that involved food. So, I devised a solution. I kept my freezer stocked with homemade cupcakes. In a moment's notice, I could whip one out, ice it, and head to a birthday party, special event, or just a spur-of-the-moment playdate. Bakeries are rarely nut-free facilities, and I hated asking parents how carefully they had prepared their baked goods—because I feared they weren't that careful. So, my solution worked great.

Until it didn't.

When Parker turned five, he became acutely aware of the fact that he was different. He wanted to eat what everyone else was eating and didn't care when we told him nuts would make him sick. (We had yet to tell him the severity of his allergy so as not to frighten him.) He assumed a nut would give him a tummy ache, and that seemed worth it. In his mind, we were withholding store-bought cakes from him, and he was over it.

So, he took matters into his own hands.

Everything unfolded at his classmate's birthday party. It was a typical rendezvous at a trampoline park. After his fellow kindergarteners were bounced out and sufficiently exhausted, they walked their wobbly legs into the designated party room. It was one long table that seated over 20 children. My son chose the farthest chair at one end and, once he was settled, I brought him his cupcake. Neatly packed in a perfectly sized Tupperware case, I placed it right next to his drink and slice of pizza.

I meandered back to the opposite end of the room and struck up a conversation with another mom. A few minutes passed, and the birthday boy's mom approached me.

"Parker told me he doesn't have a nut allergy anymore and that he can eat the birthday cake I brought! That is so exciting!"

I immediately tilted my head and gazed down the long table at my son sitting in the very last seat. He, too, was peering down the same expanse, staring back at me, knowing he had been caught but desperately hoping what he had declared to the birthday mom was now true. We locked eyes. In an instant, I nonverbally communicated loud and clear with a don't-you-dare-eat-that-birthday-cake look. He got the message and reached for the Tupperware.

I smiled politely at the birthday mom while simultaneously attempting to block out the scenarios of what could have happened if she had not inadvertently warned me.

That night we sat Parker down and reminded him what happened to his fingers the day he picked up pecans in the backyard. We explained that when a nut touches his skin, that part will immediately swell up. Then we asked him a question.

"If a nut touches the inside of your throat, what will your throat do?"

"It'll swell up," he replied. Then, after a few seconds, with his eyebrows furrowed, he followed up with his own question.

"How will I breathe if my throat swells up?"

My husband and I sat there for a moment and let the words sink in and penetrate his little mind.

"You won't be able to," said my husband.

The lightbulb went off. He understood.

Eating a nut could kill him.

It was a lot for a five-year-old to process. Even at that tender age, he ached to be like everyone else. He longed for the store-bought cake, not wanting to tote along something homemade. Though I worked hard to make his cupcakes look special by piping the icing high and adding sprinkles, it didn't matter. He felt denied and didn't understand why.

In the last chapter, we considered the question of God's care for us. In this one, let's look at another one we often contemplate in the in-between: Can you help me understand? This one is especially difficult when what we are waiting for is something good.

Why can't I get married or have this career or bear a child or be healed? Or why can't You do this wonderful thing for my loved one or fix this terrible situation? What could possibly be wrong with it? We see those around us with the very thing we desire and can't figure out why it would be a yes for them and a no for us.

We want the store-bought cake.

But what we don't realize is sometimes those store-bought cakes are at the very least a less-than-ideal choice, and at the most, horribly detrimental. And, like Parker, we don't always have the full picture.

In the book of Isaiah, it says this:

"'For my thoughts are not your thoughts, neither are your ways my ways,' declares the Lord" (Isaiah 55:8).

What does that mean? It means that sometimes our most sound logic is wrong. Sometimes our most trusted gut feeling is off. Sometimes what has always been good is now suddenly bad. And sometimes our greatest desires are downright detrimental to our souls.

There is also one more reason.

Sometimes suffering is for our good.

There. I said it. I don't want to admit it or embrace it, but it's true. We go to great lengths to avoid suffering and look like idiots to a watching world if we don't. But what if suffering could be for our good?

I remember the first time I learned this lesson.

A few months after my first son was born, I entered a season of debilitating anxiety. It felt like it came out of nowhere, and it wasn't postpartum related. Rather, it centered around the death of my father.

My dad died when I was a freshman in high school. He had a brain tumor that went undiagnosed for a while. He went to his primary care physician multiple times with legitimate concerns but was always told he was fine. Finally, after trying a different doctor, he was correctly diagnosed. At that point, however, it was too late to treat it, and he passed away a year later. For whatever reason, I didn't begin to process his death until I was in my mid-thirties and trying to care for a newborn baby.

My body underwent numerous changes as I navigated my first pregnancy. Being new to starting a family, I took note of each change and wondered if each one was normal. I regularly asked my doctor if I was okay and got the same response: "You are fine."

Little did I know, and months of therapy later, that I equated a stamp of approval from a doctor with a death wish. Like my dad, if a doctor told me I was fine, I assumed it was only because he was missing something, and I was going to die.

Irrational, I know. But that was how I had processed my father's diagnosis as a 13-year-old girl. No one explained it to me otherwise. So, I tucked away that logic as a teenager and then relied on it as an adult.

The anxiety slowly and innocuously began during my pregnancy. Though I had a textbook pregnancy, I had never experienced such rapid and continual changes in my body and questioned every nuance along the way. Each positive assurance from my doctor subconsciously increased my stress level. Little by little my fears were mounting. By the time I gave birth, I was a nervous wreck and didn't know why. And my postpartum experience only added to the alarm bells in my mind. At this point, I was confident every bodily change was the beginning of the end and that death was around the corner. Nothing my doctor said calmed my fears. I was sure he was missing something catastrophic. I was a hypochondriac in my finest hour.

The anxiety was fierce. The panic attacks were without warning. The slightest twinge in my body sent me spiraling. If someone complained of an ailment, I was sure I felt it too. I was living in a state of terror and didn't know why.

As the first few months ticked by, I turned to God. I knew I was in over my head. But I realized quickly I was face-to-face with a crisis of faith. I had been a Christian for over ten years at that point. I had been to seminary and had a decade of full-time ministry under my belt. Of course I turned to God, right?

But something was different this time.

I had never asked God for something so big before. I truly felt like my life was dependent on Him intervening, and for the first time in my relationship with Him, I wondered if He was big enough to handle it.

Like I said, the panic attacks came on quickly and with little warning. It was like there was a little teapot in my brain filled with fear, and the slightest thing caused it to tip over, spilling into my mind and then quickly spreading throughout my body. Within a matter of seconds, I was shaking uncontrollably, struggling to get a breath, and terrified beyond belief. I couldn't logically grasp how God could be fast enough to prevent the fear from pouring out.

I had been saying (and I thought believing) that God could do anything. I had touted that mantra with full confidence. The problem was I had only dealt with things that were smaller, more manageable. This felt HUGE. I didn't want to say it out loud, but deep down I wasn't sure He could help me.

And that frightened me.

What if all these years I had built a life on God only to find out God wasn't big enough when I really needed Him?

My in-between began with a jolt. After my first panic attack, I was thrust into a desperate situation and knew I couldn't help myself. I begged for help. I cried out to Him. Weeks went by with nothing but fear overtaking me. Where are You, God? I don't understand what is happening to me! I scoured the Word. Mostly in the Psalms. I searched for comfort, answers, peace… anything.

And then one day I read Psalm 40:1-3.

"I waited patiently for the Lord; he turned to me and heard my cry. He lifted me out of the slimy pit, out of the mud and mire; he set my feet on a rock and gave me a firm place to stand. He put a new song in my mouth, a hymn of praise to our God. Many will see and fear and put their trust in him."

I resonated with this passage immediately. I was in a pit! A slimy one filled with mud and mire. And oh, how I wanted to have my feet set on a rock with a firm place to stand. I longed for a new song to be in my mouth.

I pulled out a notecard and scribbled these verses on it. I began to read them over and over again. First thing in the morning, last thing at night, and many times in between.

At first, I read them longingly. This would be so wonderful! I ached to be out of the pit. As these verses trickled down into my heart, I began to ask God questions. Can you pull me out of the pit? Can you set my feet on a rock? Can you give me a firm place to stand and put a new song in my mouth?

I wanted to believe He could, but I just wasn't sure. My anxiety was rough and real. Weeks went by with me reading this notecard and asking the same questions. Finally, I reached a point of decision. I had been told for years that God's Word could be trusted—that it was true and reliable. Therefore, if that was the case, then *yes,* He can pull me out of this pit, set my feet on a rock, give me a firm place to stand, and put a new song in my mouth.

I realized I was either going to take God at His Word, or I wasn't.

I was terrified not to believe it. I was doing everything I possibly could to overcome my angst, and nothing was working. I was in therapy but was still a hot mess. So, if God's Word wasn't true, then what else could I lean on? Something bigger than myself had to help me, and this was my only option. So, I chose to believe it.

I continued reading that notecard every day, and slowly, without knowing when, my questions became statements. Now, instead of saying, "Can you...", I started saying, "I know You can..."

I know you can pull me out of this pit.

I know you can set my feet on a rock.

I know you can give me a firm place to stand.

I know you can put a new song in my mouth.

More weeks went by with this new mantra. My heart was changing. I could feel it. My faith was growing. Not by my might or muster, but simply because He was doing it in me.

Several months went by, and I felt my mantra shift again. My confidence had grown even more. Now, every time I read the notecard, I said this:

Thank you that one day you will pull me out of this pit.

Thank you that one day you will set my feet on a rock.

Thank you that one day you will give me a firm place to stand.

Thank you that one day you will put a new song in my mouth.

I had no clue how He was going to do this, but I was confident He would. I wasn't sure if I would experience any of this while still living on earth, but I was firmly convinced that one day my feet were going to stand on solid ground again. And the most amazing thing of all is I reached this place of confidence almost a year before I actually experienced it.

Yes, almost a year.

I continued to struggle with panic attacks as I transitioned from "Can you...?" to "I know you can..." to "Thank you that you will...". I kept praying this passage over and over, even though my circumstances were barely budging. My in-between felt long. My steps out of this season were so incremental I could not and did not notice them. Yet I was able to wake up and thank Him for what I trusted He would do one day.

It felt terribly contradictory.

I literally put all my eggs in one basket, as the saying goes. And my one basket was His Word. I chose to focus on it as much as possible and not let my circumstances convince me otherwise.

Then one day I realized I had gone a few days without being afraid. Then a few more days. Then a few weeks. I truly pictured Him slowly but surely raising me up out of that pit and gently but firmly, establishing a new foundation for me to stand on. The tune of the new song was so faint at first, but in time it grew into a melody of peace and joy that spread throughout me.

I spent about two and a half years in that place. But eventually my in-between came to an end, and I felt restored. At first, I didn't understand why I had needed to go through that. Yes, I needed to process my dad's death, but did it have to be that long? And so hard? And so full of suffering? Surely there could have been an easier way. I did not understand it at the time.

But God's ways are higher than mine. His

thoughts are higher than mine. His ways are higher than mine. And what He had planned for me was something I would need for years to come. He taught me how to take Him at His Word. He tuned my heart to hear Scripture over circumstances. He gave me the gift of faith.

That might sound simple on paper, but it is huge in real life. In walking the road of contradiction between my circumstances and Psalm 40, I forged a faith that ran deep. It took months for those verses to penetrate the long and lengthy parts of my soul. I needed time for them to seep into the tiny fissures that were scattered throughout my fragile, fearful heart.

During this in-between, God felt silent yet profoundly loud at the same time. I begged for my circumstances to change and was met with a whisper so quiet that most days I couldn't hear it. Yet, His Word was shouting from the rooftops that healing was around the corner. I lived with that dissonance for quite some time.

In the end, though, He was faithful. He saw me through it. And my faith was permanently changed as a result. I learned a lesson I have relied upon so many times since then. I didn't understand my in-between at the time, but that was because I didn't have the full picture. Only God knew the challenges that would lie ahead for me in the years to come, and He wanted me best prepared for them by learning how to trust His Word.

It was yet another example of why being in a partnership with Him was so important. I needed Him to lead me through that season on His timetable in order to soak in every last lesson. I could never have walked that road of my volition!

We are not promised an easy life. No one glides through effortlessly, in a constant state of bliss. No, Jesus said we would have troubles (John 16:33). But He prepares us for them. And makes us better through them.

The remarkable part of this story is I had hope that I would be healed long before I was. God's Word said I would be pulled out of that pit, and I knew if it didn't happen in my lifetime, it would happen for eternity. And though I wanted it now, it wasn't any less comforting to know it might not happen till later. A promise is a promise, and I was so grateful I had one to stand on.

I would never have chosen that path, but I am glad I walked it. And I can say that for other areas of my life too.

I did not go to the graduate school where I had hoped. And I am so glad.

I am not married to who I thought I was going to marry. And I am so glad.

I am not living in the city I thought I would live in. And I am so glad.

We don't have to understand our seasons

of waiting. Especially while we are in them. But we can trust He does.

God's thoughts are higher than mine. His ways are higher than mine. His purposes are higher than mine. And His ability to manage all of this is infinitely higher than mine.

And I am so glad.

Lord, there is so much I don't understand about this season of waiting. But I want to take you at your Word and trust that because your thoughts and ways are higher than mine, I can know you are still very much in control. Help me do this. Increase my faith. But as I wait, is there anything you can help me understand? Please open my eyes to what can make sense at this point. And help me trust you with what doesn't. Amen

Chapter Five

Have You Forgotten Me?

My husband forgot my 29th birthday. So did my mom. I don't think anyone I know remembered it, but that is probably because this was before social media birthday reminders kept us on track. But I can willingly extend grace to anyone in my life at that time because I actually forgot it too. You see, that particular birthday fell eight days after my wedding. It wasn't until I was flying home from my honeymoon that I caught sight of a newspaper across the aisle and was stunned to see that warmly familiar month and day printed across the top.

Nobody likes to be forgotten. Even when there are lots of good reasons why. There is something about going unnoticed that makes you feel puny. Unimportant.

Possibly unloved. And when it comes to our relationship with God, it feels downright confusing. God, who is omniscient, omnipresent, and omnipotent, cannot possibly forget us, right? How can He know the number of hairs on our head (Matthew 10:30), the number of days we will have on this earth (Job 14:5), and even the number of tears we have shed (Psalm 56:8, TLB) and yet seem to forget about our daily lives?

This is another question we wrestle with in the in-between.

Have you forgotten me?

Silence, difficulties, unfulfilled dreams, and waiting cannot help but lock arms and march right into the assumption that God does not remember us. Circumstances are like megaphones sometimes. I know this all too well from the season when my husband walked through a nine-month stretch of unemployment. At the time, I was homeschooling my kids and didn't work outside the home. So, let me rephrase that:

We walked through a nine-month stretch with zero income.

The setting was 2020. Need I say more? I can safely assume everyone around the world equates 2020 with one word: Covid. And, as I am sure you remember, that was not the year to be looking for a job. My husband had left a very difficult work situation at the tail end of 2019, fully expecting to find another job quickly. One month turned into two, and then somewhere in that third month, a worldwide pandemic shockingly took over.

Needless to say, the job market came to a screeching halt.

Weeks went by with absolutely nothing on the horizon. No one was even interviewing! It was truly as if the world had stopped spinning.

Except it didn't.

We still had a mortgage and bills and kids to take care of. Yet when I say there were no prospects, I mean there were no prospects. Granted, my husband was looking for a church staff position. So, that slice of the job market was particularly closed because people were not gathering in public. Rightfully so, churches were all saying the same thing: we aren't hiring right now. Everything was on hold until some semblance of normalcy began to resurface. It was discouraging, to say the least.

Hindsight is always helpful, but when you are in the midst of a situation, you don't have access to that tool. No one knew how long Covid would last. No one had any idea when the job market and life as we had known it were going to resume. Or if it would resume as we had known it.

Was this pandemic ever going to end?

Was he ever going to find a job?

This season of waiting only lasted nine months, but even at eight months we were still looking out to an empty horizon. But though this in-between was short, it was rife with uncertainty, angst, and silence. Many a day we questioned if God had forgotten us. Yet, what I learned later (in hindsight!) was that we were very much at the forefront of His mind.

We just couldn't see it.

We learned some powerful lessons during this stint of unemployment, and I am eager to share them with you. As I do, though, you will probably wonder why I had thought God had forgotten us. But isn't that often the case in these situations? We become so fixated on what we want that we miss out on what we receive. And I received a lot. I just didn't see it clearly until I was looking through the backward lens of a life already lived.

This chapter is a little different. Instead of working up to the main point, I want to lead with it: You are not forgotten. There is no fancy or earth-shattering way to explain it. There are no verses that require an understanding of Hebrew or Greek to fully grasp them. I don't have a surprise ending. The truth is plain and simple.

God has not forgotten you.

My hope for you as you hear my story

(which is broken into three stories) is that God will use it to demonstrate how He is at work in your life. And maybe you will catch a glimpse of this work without the aid of looking back in time. Here's a sneak peek of what's to come in my story. (And I share this only to show the magnitude of what He did amidst the anguish over how I thought He wasn't doing anything.)

I cried out to God, and He faithfully answered—I just didn't see it (at first).

God reached out to me, but because I wasn't looking for it, I misunderstood it (at first).

The assumption that God has forgotten us often boils down to one or both of these scenarios. We miss how He is responding to us and/or we miss how He is reaching out to us. So, may I make a suggestion? Let me encourage you to stop reading for a moment and pray. Ask God to open your eyes, ears, mind, and heart to ways He is already at work in and around you.

Because the truth of the matter is this: you are not forgotten.

Remember how I learned to take God at His Word in the last chapter? Here is the fruit of that lesson learned. This is my first of three stories about our unemployment.

My boys were in 8th and 5th grade at this time, so they were old enough to grasp that Dad didn't have a job, but young enough that they didn't comprehend the magnitude of it. It was like we were all on a journey together as a family, yet they were only carrying empty suitcases. We, as the parents, held (juggled, heaved, dragged) the weighted contents for them. As we should have.

Once the pandemic hit, the reality of finding a job quickly slipped through our fingers like soft sand. Along with it went our sense of control and confidence in the situation. It felt like overnight our life took a bleak, sharp turn in a very unpleasant direction.

But I knew I could take God at His Word. I had already learned that lesson!

My husband and I asked Him to lead us to something we could stand on. Something our boys could stand on. I don't remember who landed on this first, but one of us brought Proverbs 3:5-6 to the table.

"Trust in the Lord with all your heart and lean not on your own understanding; in all your ways acknowledge him, and he will make your paths straight."

It is a very familiar passage that has been cross-stitched, stenciled, and framed ad nauseum. Though I don't say that negatively! There is a good reason for it. But when something becomes commonplace, it is in danger of sounding like background noise. It becomes one of those I-know-those-verses-but-don't-really-know-those-verses kind of verses. Truthfully, I didn't really know those verses until this point in time.

During this season in our family's life, we were in the habit of praying together at night before bed. So we decided to share this wisdom nugget with them. We told the boys we could trust these words, stand on them, and wait on them. And we did. Most nights we read this before prayer, asking God to make our path straight. In doing so, we noticed three parts to these verses.

1. <u>Trust in the Lord with all your heart</u>

The more we read this with them, the more it sank down into our hearts. Questions naturally bubbled up from within us. Were my husband and I trusting Him with all of our hearts or just part of it? Were we relying on other things, including Him, or just Him? We spent time examining our hearts in ways we never had before.

2. <u>Lean not on your own understanding</u>

Were we leaning on our understanding? This one pricked my heart every time I began to worry. If I allowed my circumstances to dictate my understanding, I tripped over trouble. If I gave in to the empty email inbox, the lack of phone calls from future employers, or the increasing spread of Covid, I knew I was leaning on my own understanding. I was making sense of our situation separate from God's intervention.

3. <u>In all your ways acknowledge Him</u>

Were we acknowledging Him in all our ways? On the surface, this means recognizing His existence. I think we were doing that. But a deeper understanding of this word means to know Him. To know His holiness, authority, and lordship. Another translation of this verse is "in all your ways submit to him." Did our actions, even our simple, everyday ones, fall in line with His holiness, authority, and lordship? Were we living lives that honored Him? Were we engaged in a partnership and not a religion or a relationship with Him? Again, more self-reflection was required.

Over time, we discovered another way to organize this passage. We divided it into two main categories: our job and God's job. We have three responsibilities; God has one. If we trust with our whole heart, lean not on our own minds, and acknowledge Him with our words and actions, He would make our path straight. All we wanted was a straight path, but in order to achieve that, we had to get serious about our heart, mind, and actions.

Now, please do not mistake my words for any type of works-based mentality. God has never been a puppet that we command through our actions. Our three responsibilities are not tapping their feet, waiting for God to do His part. Rather, God uses those three areas to shape our hearts and strengthen us so we can better navigate the hard right turns, U-turns, and sudden stops in life. It is to our benefit to follow His instructions.

Proverbs 3:5-6 became the hook we hung our faith on. It kept us steadily anchored. By regularly checking our hearts, our minds, and our actions, we were able to maintain a posture of partnership that was ready to receive what God had for us. Because, as it turns out, it was much more than a job that He had in store.

But we couldn't see that at the time.

In the moment all we could focus on was a job. And the lack thereof. We couldn't see the gentle shaping of our lives as we did our best to move our hearts, minds, and actions in His direction. We didn't notice that our faith was steadily growing even in the face of discouraging circumstances. We missed what God was doing in us, but that didn't stop Him from working.

We were not forgotten.

At one point along the way, we told God we would take the first job that was offered. At this point, my husband had branched out beyond ministry roles, willing to do whatever. His resume was scattered about, and we chose to trust that whatever came first we would take. God knew our financial situation, and we trusted He didn't want us to be picky.

The first nibble we got from the resume bait was a role he did not want. It made our hearts

When Waiting Feels Like Withholding

sink at the possibility of moving our family for a position that was less than desired. But we trusted and said yes. The employer said he would email some paperwork and, once it was filled out, we could move forward. We waited for him to send it. Every week or two he would say it was coming, but something always happened to divert his attention.

More waiting. More silence. More yuck.

After a couple of months, we got the second nibble. It was a church staff position that we were very interested in. It was a great job! They seemed interested in us; we expressed interest in return, and then it went radio silent. After several weeks of silence, we assumed they had filled the position.

Then, out of nowhere, two months later, we heard from them again. They explained that they had had to reassess hiring due to the pandemic but were now ready to move forward again if we were still interested. We excitedly said yes.

Suddenly, our season of waiting was over. Once we signed the dotted line everything quickly fell into place. Within ten days we bought a house, sold a house, packed up and moved. *Everything* was a straight path. It was so fast we got whiplash leaving our old city and moving to the new one.

(And, PS, the day after my husband was hired, we finally got the paperwork from the first job. My husband happily declined.)

Over and over again we told our boys God would make our path straight. And the more we said it, the more we believed it. Our faith had been steadily growing. Choosing to put Proverbs 3:5-6 into daily practice steadily sustained us and shaped us. And it spoke volumes to our friends and neighbors when it all came to fruition. God made Himself known through our situation.

But, like I said, we didn't appreciate any of that until it was over.

So, that's my first story. Here's the second.

A few weeks into our unemployment, I got a card in the mail from a friend that knew of our situation. In it was a gift card to a local grocery store. I was so touched. How thoughtful! A week or so later I got another card with a similar gift. Again, I was grateful.

Then, a week later, I got a card from someone who didn't know my husband was unemployed. Her card said God had laid it on her heart to mail us a check. I was touched, grateful, and totally surprised!

And then I got another card. And another.

You can see where this is going.

Every couple of weeks we would get a gift in the mail from someone. Sometimes it was from someone who knew our situation, and sometimes it wasn't. But the message was the same: God nudged me to send this to you. It was just enough to meet our needs until the next card.

I started keeping a list so I could send out thank-you notes at the end of this nine-month journey. In the end, it totaled over $11,000.

And we never received another card after my husband got a job.

You would think I would have been overwhelmed with God's provision, feeling close in heart to Him. But sadly, I wasn't. Yes, I was grateful for every gift. And I recognized that they were from Him, but I wanted employment. That was all I could focus on. I remember one time a check came in the mail, and I shook my fist in the air and said through tears, "I don't want another check! I want a job!"

Yuck. I cringe writing those words.

God had a straight path for us that would not open up for a few months. But He sustained us until that point. He was faithful. He was kind. We were not forgotten. I just missed it.

I was so focused on what I wanted, that I didn't notice what I received.

Ugh.

The final story takes place in my backyard. This was the turning point for me. Though God was with us through every step of this journey, I didn't fully embrace it until this moment. It was beautiful. I will try to describe it, though I may not do it justice. Sometimes when God speaks to you, it is only meant for you. You can retell it later, but somehow you won't be able to fully capture or express it the way you want to.

But here goes...

My heart was heavy that day as I sat on my back porch. I had been on the verge of tears for the umpteenth time. We were entering the seventh month of unemployment, and there wasn't a prospect in sight. (This was during the radio-silent period of the second job opportunity. The time when we assumed they had hired someone else.)

I went outside intentionally to connect with God. I love sitting still in the early morning hours and listening to His creation wake up to a new day. My attention that morning, though, was squarely fixed on the large pecan tree in the middle of the yard. It loomed large and kept vying for my attention. It sat motionless. No squirrels were scrambling on it, no birds were perching in it, not even a leaf was quivering near it. It was eerily and perfectly still. I tried to refocus my mind to pray or worship, but inevitably, within minutes, I was drawn back to a tree that appeared to be frozen in time. A tree that mirrored my life.

How long, God?

When will he get a job?

Why won't You provide one?

Tears were brimming when I sighed loudly and looked up at the sky. What I saw took me by surprise and instantly stole my attention.

Clouds were rapidly racing across the sky. They were silently and majestically engaged in a mad dash to the other end of my peripheral view. I couldn't believe it. How had I missed this? I had been sitting for over 15 minutes, riveted by a tree that was not allowing a single leaf to wave while some mighty, yet completely muted, force of wind was powerfully moving clouds directly above me. How could things be moving overhead, yet at a standstill right in front of me?

How is that even possible?

At that moment, the silence I felt from God was broken. I knew what He was communicating through those clouds. It was a visual reminder of Him at work in my life. I had been so fixated on what wasn't happening (the tree), that I nearly missed what *was* (the racing clouds)! Though I felt painfully paused, I realized He wasn't. In fact, He had never stopped moving.

The tears that had been gathering finally spilled over. Not out of sadness, but gratitude. In that moment, nothing had outwardly changed with my situation, yet my heart had found a place of rest.

In that moment I knew I was not forgotten.

A month and a half after God spoke through the wind in my backyard, my husband was gainfully employed again. And once we learned why they had been so silent after first reaching out to us, I fully appreciated the moving clouds. God had been at work that day I sat outside. We just couldn't see it yet.

Remember the two points I made at the beginning of the chapter? Let's revisit them.

I cried out to God, and He faithfully answered—I just didn't see it (at first).

God reached out to me, but because I wasn't looking for it, I misunderstood it (at first).

Using the promise of Proverbs 3:5-6 as an anchor of hope, I cried out to God, praying He would make a straight path for us. And while He faithfully answered that, He also taught me how to turn my heart, mind, and actions toward Him. He shaped my character and grew my faith. I just missed it (at first).

God reached out to me through checks and other provision, but because I was fixated on a job, I misunderstood Him (at first). So, He stilled a tree and forcefully blew a massive mess of clouds overhead to get my attention. And He got it.

Have you been so fixated on what you want that you haven't noticed what you have already received?

Once again, sit quietly. Ask God to show you. Look for the clouds overhead.

I was not forgotten, and neither are you.

Chapter Six

Are You Punishing Me?

Some things don't have to be taught.

At an early age, children decide for themselves what they like and don't like. No one has to teach them to want toys or cookies or smartphones (sigh). Similarly, they need no guidance for how to react when someone takes said toys, cookies, or smartphones from them. Very quickly they learn to do what feels good and to avoid what feels yucky.

Logic, or simply trying to make sense of things, comes naturally.

Now, logic can certainly be distorted and rationalized, leading to something illogical. But the concept of logic itself is not something that is taught. Our brains are wired to make sense of things. At a young age, we learn that touching a hot stove hurts. Therefore, don't touch a hot stove. Don't pinch your brother because you will get pinched back. And don't tattle on a friend in school or everyone will hate you.

I can't say we always heed our logic, though.

One of my happiest memories as a teenager was going to Hilton Head Island, South Carolina, on vacation. My bestie, Suzanne, went with her family every summer, and I would tote along with them. It was a 10-hour drive from our hometown in Kentucky, so every year, Suzanne and I prepared adequately for the trip. We would walk to Walgreens, snatch a thin plastic bag from the Brach's Pick-A-Mix Candy stand and fill it up with butterscotch discs, lemon drops and other delicious treats. We would weigh our bags, drop our cash on the counter, and head back home. Then we would proceed to eat that candy for the next 10 hours. And every summer, my stomach hurt on the first evening of our trip.

We might not listen to logic's warnings, but nonetheless it is there.

According to the dictionary, logic is defined as follows: a particular method of reasoning or argumentation. Like I said, sometimes our methods are faulty. They stem from insecurities, lies, assumptions, or misunderstandings. But the fact that we innately form a method in our minds is the point I want to make.

In reference to our discussion on waiting, it looks a little like this: The longer we spend in the in-between, the more desperate our brains are to make sense of it. Our neurons are firing left and right trying to piece together why we are in this particular situation. We wrestle with what the Bible says and what others have told us about God, and we struggle to reconcile our pain with His love.

But because we are wired for logic, we can't rest until we have an answer. So, we pepper God with a series of questions and statements, searching to understand how love and suffering fit together.

Lord, don't you care?

Can you help me understand?

Have you forgotten me?

If we still can't make sense of our situation, we often, by power of elimination, arrive at the next assumption:

Are you punishing me?

If we believe God loves us and that His ways are good and true, then when we are faced with a painful season of waiting, we can't help but wonder if our situation is our fault. Have we done something wrong? Is there sin in our lives? Is there a lesson that needs to be learned? When the disappointment or the longing or the pain stretches on, our minds drift into the territory of punishment. And we shouldn't be surprised by that. We aren't the first ones to follow that train of thought.

Remember Job? The guy in the Old Testament who loved God and was minding his own business when he was struck with one catastrophe after another? If you are not familiar with his story, a thief stole his donkeys and camels, his sheep and servants burned in a fire, his kids died in a house that collapsed on itself, and then he was covered in wicked sores (Job 1-2).

Those kinds of tragedies.

His friends learned of this terrible turn of events and gathered as one to make sense of the situation and offer some assistance. After conferring, they unanimously agreed on their assessment.

It was Job's fault.

His buddy Eliphaz began the discussion:

"Consider now: Who, being innocent, has ever perished? Where were the upright ever destroyed?" (Job 4:7)

Do you follow his method of reasoning? He clearly makes the argument that the innocent don't perish and the upright don't get destroyed. Therefore, if someone is perishing or being destroyed... well... you can connect the dots.

Up next is Bildad. He also takes a not-so-subtle approach.

"Surely God does not reject one who is blameless" (Job 8:20).

Translation: You aren't blameless, Job.

Finally, the third amigo, Zophar, tries to offer some advice about what Job should do, now that he is in this horrible predicament.

"Yet if you devote your heart to him and stretch out your hands to him, if you put away the sin that is in your hand and allow no evil to dwell in your tent, then, free of fault, you will lift up your face; you will stand firm and without fear" (Job 11:13-15).

In other words, c'mon Job, just own up and quit sinning. Then God will get rid of this painful trial.

Even Job's own wife was convinced he had messed up. Her advice was to give up altogether (Job 2:9). In short, there was not a person in his life who didn't assume Job had done *something*.

The problem was Job was not in the wrong, and he knew it.

How quickly we can assume our mistakes have caught up with us and translated into punishment. Now, pain is not always a result of punishment, and suffering is not always due to sin. Sometimes, as with Job, it is something far deeper—a story God is writing that we cannot see. Yet it's so hard to trust that there is a deeper story when we have only experienced the surface of it.

We can't fathom why God would allow such painful circumstances in our lives. And not to mention, we have been trained since childhood to associate pain with punishment. If we did something wrong (and got caught), we faced negative consequences that hurt. So, if life hurts as an adult, then we must have done something wrong.

Again, simple logic.

So, can your in-between be a result of punishment? Let's start with a more basic question: Does God punish? The short answer is yes.

I have been taught that God is like a two-sided coin. On one side, He is perfectly just. On the other side, He is perfectly loving. The tension between the two is reconciled in the death of Jesus and is best captured in Romans 5:8.

"But God demonstrates His own love for us in this: while we were still sinners, Christ died for us."

God is perfectly just and cannot disregard our sin. It would contradict His nature not to require payment for our wrongdoings. But because He is also perfectly loving, He provided a way for that payment. He sent His Son to die in our place.

So, does God punish for sin? Yes. He would not be perfectly just if He didn't. But has He lovingly provided a substitute to spare us that punishment? Yes. It is a big, fancy word called propitiation. The death of Jesus satisfies the requirement that the holiness of God requires.

In light of that super-fast theological lesson, we can now answer the *really* pressing question. Can our in-between be a result of punishment? And the answer is unequivocally no. The apostle John settled this matter a long time ago in the form of a letter written to first-century believers. He writes:

"My little children, I am writing these things to you so that you may not sin. But if anyone does sin, we have an advocate with the Father, Jesus Christ the righteous. He is the propitiation for our sins, and not for ours only but also for the sins of the whole world" (1 John 2:1-2, ESV).

Nothing about your waiting, longing, hoping, or dreaming is a form of punishment. He is holy and cannot tolerate sin, but your sins have already been paid for. Propitiation is a word worth cheering about.

Rest easy. God is not punishing you.

Now, having said that, there is the matter of discipline. Discipline feels similar to punishment, but is different by definition. It can look like punishment and feel like punishment, but it is not punishment. And we need to be careful not to confuse the two.

Punishment is the requirement necessary to pay for our sins, and it was satisfied with Christ's death on the cross. Discipline occurs when sin sidetracks us and God is working in a way to get us back on track. It emphasizes learning and growth, aimed at helping us make better choices in the future.

Discipline (though sometimes painful) is positive.

God most definitely disciplines us. Why? Because, like the coin analogy, He is both fully just and fully loving. Together His holiness and love direct His actions and intentions toward us, keeping our good at the forefront of His mind. Note everything that we gain from God's discipline:

"...God disciplines us for our good, in order that we may share in his holiness. No discipline seems pleasant at the time, but painful. Later on, however, it produces a harvest of righteousness and peace for those who have been trained by it" (Hebrews 12:10b-11).

Discipline allows us to share in His holiness, and it produces a harvest of righteousness and peace in us. Make no mistake, God disciplines us for our good.

Remember that season of anxiety I mentioned in chapter 4? During that time, I distinctly recall one of my prayer times. My request had not changed. I still longed for healing, help, relief. But this time, as I prayed, a relationship that had been strained crossed my mind. I knew God was nudging me to forgive her. It was an unpleasant exchange from a long time ago, but I had stuffed it down and put it out of my mind. She didn't live near me, so I wasn't confronted with it often. But the exchange had been festering. The roots of bitterness had been growing.

The nudge felt out of left field, though. I reminded God I needed His attention squarely focused on my anxiety. I could deal with that person later. But He didn't budge. It was a showdown for sure and because of His kindness toward me (Romans 2:4), He wasn't going to back down.

It wasn't until I made that relationship right in my heart did God start attending to my anxiety. He was disciplining me for my good knowing bitterness would never serve me well. I learned a powerful lesson through that experience. God deeply cares about the sin in our lives and will go to great lengths to bring it to our attention.

Okay, let's summarize what we have learned so far. Punishment and discipline may feel the same but by definition are different. Your in-between is not because God is punishing you. Scripture settles that. But it could be because He is disciplining you. On the previous page we read Hebrews 12:10-11, but now try reading it in context (v. 4-11) and examine your life in light of it. Try sitting with Psalm 139:23-24, also. Allow God to use these passages to speak to you about discipline, if need be.

In short, punishment is off the table, though discipline might be an issue. But there is a third option we need to consider too. A third option that easily rears its head during seasons of waiting.

For more years than I care to admit, I have longed for a speaking career. I realize you may not resonate with that dream in any way. Public speaking is most people's greatest fear. But not me. I love to teach. And, believe it or not, the seed for this desire was planted before I even was a Christian.

In high school, my mom worked for a seminar company that partnered with the Holiday Inn hotel chain. Speakers would rent conference rooms hoping to broadcast their latest technique, business endeavor, or round of advice to a roomful of eager attendees. My mom oversaw the housekeeping and administration tasks for each seminar. She would position herself outside the room and handle registration, nametags, and refreshments for the participants, while also managing the speaker's book sales. During the summer months, I sometimes tagged along as her assistant.

I was fascinated by the speakers. What an interesting and exciting job that allowed them to tour the country, sharing some exciting ideas in hopes of selling their must-have book. Best of all, they got to stay in Holiday Inns, a highlight in my young opinion! A future career evolved in my mind. How hard could it be to plan a speech, get on stage, and deliver it? Traveling, speaking, and sharing something worthwhile seemed like an ideal career.

It was during those poignant high school summers that the seed of a speaker's ambition began to root itself in my heart. So, as graduation approached, I decided on a college and a major, speech communication. I had a plan and was on my way!

But, lo and behold, a few months into my freshman year, the message of the gospel captured my heart, taking my life in a drastically different direction (see chapter 2). I spent the remainder of my college career attending every Bible study, retreat, and mission trip I could find. My interest in speech communication took a back seat to my spiritual life, but after three years, the reality of my degree took center stage again because I graduated.

Suddenly, I had no desire to hop on the Holiday Inn tour bus. In fact, my only goal was to keep learning about Jesus. My college pastor wisely suggested I sign up to work for a year as a college ministry intern, and I took his advice. I left my southern roots and cruised out west, to a university in Arizona. With only a few years of Christianity under my belt and a few months of college behind me, I gave it everything I had.

I. Loved. It.

After two semesters working in college ministry, I was hooked. I marched my way to seminary and earned my master's degree with the goal of pursuing a full-time ministry career. I spent the next decade mentoring and spiritually investing in the lives of college students. My life was full.

So, when did the speaking dream resurface?

As anyone in full-time college ministry will tell you, speaking comes with the territory. So, as my tenure grew, so did my love of communicating. I enjoyed delving into a Bible passage and uncovering truths that could produce life change. When I experienced answered prayers, I longed to weave them into messages that inspired others to pray for themselves. I spent hours poring over Scripture, carefully crafting a message that would be easy to grasp and would apply to their lives.

My speech communication degree was certainly coming in handy, but not in the way I had imagined all those years ago. As my season of college ministry came to an end, I once again dreamed of becoming a speaker. But this time, my sights weren't set on the Holiday Inn circuit.

I wanted to be on the local church circuit.

The next couple of decades can be summarized in a few short sentences. I tried to establish a speaking career in all the ways I knew how. First, I expanded to include writing. Speaking and writing are two peas in the same pod of teaching, and I enjoy both. In an effort to launch either branch of this dream, I read books, went to conferences, hired a coach, had professional bio sheets made, did mail-outs, email blasts, wrote blogs and anytime I met someone in women's ministry, I would slip in somehow that I loved to teach. When social media hit the scene, I posted blogs, wrote new posts, and even tried a live teaching series. I also self-published a Bible study.

But nothing gained traction.

Sure, I had the occasional speaking opportunity here and there, and I had a smattering of blog subscribers and book sales, but nothing was consistent.

Looking back, my desire to teach and share messages from Scripture evolved without me realizing it. God had aligned my experiences in high school, captured my heart in college, prepared me through my major, and set me in motion with student ministry. He gave me opportunities that only served to fuel my desire. In hindsight, it seemed obvious that God took what seemed like random pieces of my life and, over time, fit them together perfectly.

So, why would God engineer this dream in my heart, only to withhold it from me later?

At first, I was confused. Why wouldn't God open doors for me? Why wouldn't He want me to be a Bible teacher?! Over time, my confusion morphed into varying degrees of frustration, disappointment, and bouts of jealousy. I prayed and asked God to take away the desire or fulfill it. But please don't leave me in the in-between.

Yet, I remained in that space.

I felt like a horse lined up to run a race. If you aren't familiar with horse racing, the jockeys lead their horses onto the track and into one of many individual, interconnected stalls that span the width of the track. Once inside the stall, the door shuts behind them, locking them into that small space. Within seconds, the front-facing door will fly open, and the horse will leap out of the stall and charge forward.

I felt as if God had led me onto the track and tucked me into my stall. The dream lay ahead of me, and I was eager to set out after it. I couldn't back out of the dream because the rear door had locked me in. But the front-facing door refused to open.

So I was forced to remain in that space of wanting something yet unable to pursue it or leave it behind.

My logic went into overdrive. I was determined to make sense of my situation. I truly wanted to follow Christ with my life and couldn't reconcile His love with this painful season. So somewhere along the way, I made the assumption that it had to be me. I had to be the problem. If God gave me a passion to teach and speak, then He must be withholding the opportunities from me because I was doing something wrong.

For years I searched for where I was in error. Maybe it was pride, or not enough Bible knowledge, or a lack of prayer. I felt like I was sitting in front of a safe, staring at the combination lock. My dream was locked inside, and I was determined to crack the code. I was forever rotating the dial, desperately looking for the right order of numbers. I was sure if I could be enough in those areas, if I could turn the dial with the right amount of tiny clicks, I would finally hear the "thunk" of the lock being released and the door would swing open.

But I could never find the right combination. And with each failed attempt came a stern voice of correction from within myself. A rebuke. A chastisement. An internal pronouncement that I still wasn't getting it right.

You are too prideful.

You don't pray enough.

You don't have enough knowledge.

And then after attempts to be humble, pray more, and study more, I would be berated with round two:

You are a failure at this.

You will never get this right.

It's your fault this dream has not been realized.

On and on the dialogue went. And this dialogue further cemented my attempted, yet faulty logic: Due to my own shortcomings, my dream was withheld.

I was the problem.

At the time, I thought it was a voice of godly rebuke or discipline. I pictured God shaking His head in disappointment at my inability to measure up. I imagined Him throwing His hands in the air saying, "I have to withhold this until you get it right!" It wasn't until many years later I realized this stern voice was not disciplining me for my good and trying to build me up. Rather, it was a voice full of accusations that was tearing me down.

It was the voice of condemnation.

God wasn't punishing me. I was punishing myself.

And this is the third option we must consider: condemnation. What are we doing to personally berate ourselves during our season of waiting? How are we needlessly critiquing our actions and interactions with others?

As we question God during seasons of waiting, we now know three things:

It is not punishment.

It *might* be discipline.

And it should never be condemnation.

We have an enemy that wants to steal, kill, and destroy us (John 10:10a). And his most effective weapon is lies. His job is to convince us that we don't measure up. Once he sets that faulty train of thought in motion, we push it further down the tracks of our minds. In doing so, our understanding of ourselves and of God are slowly distorted. We scold ourselves for not being good enough and then start to assume God isn't good anymore either.

Condemnation says I am a failure and will never get it right. If I allow myself to internalize that, then I will quickly personalize it. I am a failure. I won't ever get it right. And that line of thinking only spirals downward. It can lead to self-hatred, or if we are convinced that we have no worth, it causes us to operate out of insecurity and insignificance. None of these outcomes has anything to do with God. So here is the bottom line:

The enemy likes to twist and distort your logic in a way that narrows your reasoning down to one conclusion: it's your fault.

So, how do we stop this vicious cycle of self-induced punishment?

Here are a few questions that I am learning to ask myself. First, consider what thoughts are front and center and on repeat in your mind. What do you hear yourself saying? Are you cheering yourself on and giving grace to yourself when needed? Or do you tell yourself you are not good enough or that you are prone to failure? Do you see yourself as dearly loved by God and precious in His sight? Or do you dwell on past mistakes, picking them apart and critiquing your every move? Do you view your life through a lens of gratitude, or do you assume you don't deserve something or that you need to be like someone else in order to attain it? Pay attention to what tends to repeat itself. Jot your thoughts down somewhere and look at them on paper. (It really does help to see them written down.) Next, examine them considering Scripture.

Do they pass the 1 Corinthians 13:1-7 test? Are they patient, kind, honoring, and not keeping a record of wrongs? Or are they easily angered and crashing like clanging cymbals in your heart?

What about the checklist found in Galatians 5:22-23? Do your words have an undercurrent of love, joy, peace, patience, kindness, goodness, faithfulness, gentleness and self-control?

And don't forget the Ephesians 4:29 standard. Are your thoughts building you up or tearing you down?

Spend time in these passages evaluating your thought life. Weed out any condemnation and attempts to punish yourself. Condemnation doesn't do us any favors. And we don't have to listen to the enemy's subtle lies. "There is therefore no condemnation for those who are in Christ Jesus" (Romans 8:1).

Now, *that* is logic we need to learn to embrace.

God isn't punishing you. But are you punishing yourself?

As we close this chapter, be sure to direct your logic to exclude punishment, be open to learning from discipline, and to avoid condemnation on all levels. Correcting our thought patterns not only prevents us from unnecessary pain but it helps us step out of the vicious cycle of unhealthy patterns of relating to others and ourselves. Patterns that trap us and keep us stuck.

Are you ready to stop being stuck in your thinking? We have wrestled with questions that loom in the in-between but now let's discuss practical ways to move forward while waiting well.

Keep pressing on, my friend! There's even more hope on the horizon.

*Section Three:
Moving Forward
While Waiting
Well*

Chapter Seven
Unraveling Your Fixation

A watched pot never boils.

If you haven't heard that before, give it a try. It really is true. The patience it takes to stare at a pot of water until it boils is more than most people can handle. You have to look away. The wait is excruciating. Let's just say I won't be surprised if we find out one day that pots really are alive and that they secretly wait for you to look away, or better yet walk away, until they allow the water within them to rumble. Don't be fooled. They have all the power and won't budge no matter how hard you stare. It is much better if you just busy yourself around the kitchen and let the pot do its "pot magic."

Am I right?

The angst we feel in a watched pot experiment is our utter lack of control. We cannot will the water to boil any more than we can stop the bubbles once they begin to erupt. Similarly, as we wait on God, so much is out of our control. There is absolutely nothing we can do to speed God up or manipulate how He works things out. All we can do is peer over the lip of His almighty cookware and wait. But does waiting equate sitting still and trying to be patient?

What can we do in our spiritual kitchen while we wait for God to work? Cracking open a jar of spaghetti sauce or snapping stalks of pasta in half doesn't add to or take away from the boiling process. But it does help us prepare the meal. So what can we do as we wait for God to answer or resolve or provide or remove?

I am a doer. Sitting idle is torture. Even if my efforts don't produce much, it helps to know I am doing *something.*

As we move through the in-between, we must wrestle with our emotions, as we have done in the previous section of the book. But at some point, I must live my life, and so do you. I have to get out of bed, get dressed, and keep walking through my season of waiting. In this section of the book, I want to explore practical ways we can keep moving forward as we learn to wait well.

As I sit to write this chapter, I have a 14-week-old puppy staring at me. Pleading with me. Begging me to pick him up. His name is Barkley, and he is an adorable miniature schnauzer. He is all black with patches of white on his paws and beard, and he is a licker. This pup has lots of love to share. He also has monumental amounts of energy. If I were to describe him in two words, I would choose these:

A. Lot.

I am astounded at his level of speed and endurance. It is truly a sight to behold.

Due to his unending vigor, my family and I have tuned into his obsession with a small, squeaky orange ball. It is the key to wearing him out. Or at least our attempt to do so. We squeeze it to get his attention, toss it down the tile floor, and watch him race to retrieve it. The only reason this age-old game of fetch ever ends is when the ball rolls under the couch. Then the sedentary family member has to decide if the game is worth continuing.

This orange ball is Barkley's most prized possession. I truly believe his facial expression changes when he sees it. It doesn't matter where he is or what he is doing. If he hears the squeak, he knows it's game on.

The problem, though, is he becomes so focused on the ball that he becomes unaware of his surroundings. For example, one time the ball sped down the kitchen floor, passing underneath the table by shooting directly between the chair legs. Barkley followed its path with precision and proceeded to clock himself on the bottom rung of the chair. Another time, the ball whizzed down the hallway and ricocheted off a door that was slightly ajar. The ball took a hard right, causing Barkley to put on the brakes with his paws. Unfortunately, there wasn't enough time to stop, and he slid into the door.

But have no fear. He is never deterred. With a quick shake of the head, he is back in the game.

As a family, we now know we have to look out for Barkley's well-being. When we release the ball into the room, we have to predict its path. His love affair with this little orange sphere knows no bounds, and left to his own devices, he could end up with a fractured skull.

There are dangers in being fixated on something. We lose our objectivity and ability to gauge our surroundings. And sometimes we miss out on something wonderful simply because the object of our singular focus is blocking its view!

Remember that desire for a speaking and writing career I mentioned in the last chapter? It was definitely a fixation of mine for many years. I already shared the first lesson I learned from that experience with you. I punished myself, assuming I was not good enough. But coupled with my inability to "get it right" was a deeper issue. I had a problem with the dream itself. I had carefully crafted and pictured in my mind the career I wanted, and anything less than that was unacceptable. Basically, I had drawn the plans for my future and then held onto the blueprint with a vice grip.

When we get fixated on what we want, it creates tunnel vision. And who can blame us? We live in a culture of strong autonomy and individualism. When we want something, we are told unequivocally that we can have it. Just work hard, stand firm, be bold. There are a plethora of self-help books and podcasts dedicated entirely to helping you achieve your dreams. We are bombarded with messages telling us not only to live the way we want to, but that it is our right to do so.

And that's not all.

Our culture is also instant. We are regularly reminded that anything we want should be at our fingertips and readily accessible.

Want to be entertained? You can watch any movie or TV show on any device on demand. Or you can endlessly scroll social media.

Hungry? You can order food exactly how you want it, and it will be ready when you drive up, or you can have it delivered to you.

Want to go on a date? Take your pick of dating apps.

Need something? Amazon Prime.

Want to reach someone? Text.

Have a question? Google.

Want to plan a vacation, prepare for a work meeting, create a song, design a picture, or write a book? AI.

(I cringe as I write that.)

We are so accustomed to getting what we want, when we want it, and how we want it. We are fully in control of so many aspects of our lives that we forget we aren't in control of all of them. We lack patience. The muscles required to wait on God have atrophied. It is no wonder we become more and more fixated on what we want when we are denied the very things we want! We don't know what to do when our life cannot be accessed by touching a screen. But we must remember these crucial realities:

God is not an app at our disposal.

His ways cannot be googled.

His plans cannot be tailored.

And nothing about AI can help us speed up the in-between.

Dang.

I know that because I tried. Obviously, I know God is not an app, but mentally I put Him in that category sometimes. I tap my foot impatiently. I question Him. I allow my fixation to drive my emotions. I expect Him to operate with more speed and efficiency. And here is what I have learned from all of that striving:

When you live instantly, it is hard to live patiently. And without patience comes fixation.

So, yes, I get it. When we aren't acquiring what we want, we want it even more. Nothing satisfies. Contentment eludes us. And life becomes colored by lack.

But what if it doesn't have to be?

My fixation was a filter through which I saw my life, washing everything with a grayish hue. Thankfully, though, God came to my rescue, and He used a group of friends to do it.

For several years I have been involved in a small group at my church. Week after week we share our lives and spur one another on spiritually. Over time, a safe and sweet bond was formed.

Remember the voice of condemnation from the last chapter? The way I spoke so harshly to myself? These dear friends were the first ones to point that out in my life. They reminded me of God's character and how He is never cruel, punishing, or condemning. They were quick to contradict my thoughts, ones I *thought* were from God.

Through these friends, I learned to distinguish what was and wasn't God's voice. In time I was able to hear Him better. But all along the way, I was still wondering and waiting for my dream career to be fulfilled. Occasional opportunities to teach still emerged, but it was a far cry from a career. Therefore, it was a constant question I held before the Lord.

At that time, I had a job where I sat between two Bible verses. Literally. On the wall behind my desk was one of them, and framed in a bookcase in front of me was the other. I faced them physically and figuratively every day.

Behind me on a large, deep blue canvas hung Ephesians 2:10.

"For we are God's masterpiece, created in Christ Jesus to do good works, which God prepared in advance for us to do."

Before me, beautifully decorated in pastels and propped up with a miniature easel, was a print of Psalm 16:5-6.

"Lord, you alone are my portion and my cup; you make my lot secure. The boundary lines have fallen for me in pleasant places; surely I have a delightful inheritance."

I found myself pondering these two Scriptures on a regular basis. I noticed how well they complemented one another. God has good works for me to do. That is His plan. He also has boundary lines drawn for me. And within those lines is a delightful inheritance. Therefore, the good works He has planned for me fall within those boundary lines.

So why wasn't my dream one of the good works within my boundary lines?

I noticed the common thread that connects these verses is that I should expect something good. I thought that a career centered on teaching God's Word was a good thing. But it was clear that my dream was not within my boundary lines. And the lines that were drawn didn't feel very pleasant.

I did a lot of soul-searching at that desk, sandwiched between those biblical truths. I knew God's word to be true, so I wanted to figure out why my boundary lines didn't feel very pleasant. Once again, my trusted friends came to the rescue with much-needed wisdom.

One afternoon, I was sharing with them about a recent teaching opportunity I had been given. It had been a fruitful experience, and I made this statement: "That was a fun message to deliver, but I just wish I had more opportunities like this." One of my friends spoke up immediately and asked me why there was a "but" in that sentence.

"Why can't you put a period there? Why does there have to be a 'but'?" she pointed out.

She went on to explain that I couldn't appreciate what I was currently experiencing because my sights were continually set on something further down the road. A visual picture emerged in my mind. This "career" that I longed for was outside of the boundary lines that had been set for me. Yet my eyes were locked on that place, fixed beyond the boundary lines. I was contributing to my disappointment by setting my sights further than they needed to be.

I continued my soul searching with questions I needed to wrestle with: Why was this career so important to me? Why had it become a fixation? Why was my heart so singularly focused? As I sat with my musings, an answer slowly bubbled up to the surface of my mind. And this answer shed some light on my situation.

I want to be used by God. That is the truest part of my heart. And teaching is where I feel that most prominently. I have witnessed Him using a message or a conversation after an event to make a difference in someone's life, and I wanted more of *that*. But I could have *that* with or without a career. And for that matter, I could have *that* with or without actually teaching!

Wanting to be used by God did not mean I had to be a speaker or a writer.

I felt a crack in my very hardened assumption that this career was what I wanted. A shaft of light pierced through the crack, shifting my mindset in a new direction. For so long, all I wanted was the blueprint of my life that I had drawn. These simulated expectations were driving me past the bounds God had already mapped out for me.

No wonder my boundary lines didn't feel comfortable. I was trying to live outside of them.

One by one, my friends helped me see I was already achieving what I had hoped for—to be used by Him—but in ways I was not expecting. They pointed out that God was using me, but I didn't see it because it didn't fit within the painted mental picture of a career that I had envisioned. They helped me understand that my unmet expectations had created a fixation in me that continually led to disappointment. It also clouded what *was* happening.

It was a powerful truth for me. Let me restate it:

An unmet expectation can create a fixation that not only leads to disappointment, but clouds what is happening.

Fixations are dangerous if left unchecked. They fuel us in the wrong direction. And only one degree off of God's trajectory for our lives will lead to a giant chasm over time.

And even good things can become bad fixations!

In the book of Hebrews, we find the very words we need to navigate this life and remain in the center of God's trajectory. Let's unpack them together.

"Therefore, since we are surrounded by such a great cloud of witnesses, let us throw off everything that hinders and the sin that so easily entangles. And let us run with perseverance the race marked out for us, fixing our eyes on Jesus, the pioneer and perfecter of faith" (Hebrews 12:1-2a).

God wants us to remain at the center of His plans for us. Remember the good works He has planned for us in advance? (Ephesians 2:10) And the boundary lines He has placed in our lives? (Psalm 16:6) This passage speaks a similar message.

1. Fix your eyes on Jesus.

2. Run after Him.

3. Get rid of anything that interferes with that.

Let's look more closely at this race. This passage teaches me that my race requires perseverance. That means some days won't be easy. Some days I won't feel like pressing on. Some days I will be confused.

Some days, I will want to turn back or head in a different direction. And the only way to run with perseverance is to fix my eyes on Jesus.

Period.

We aren't told to glance at Jesus. The goal isn't to swivel past Him on occasion. We aren't instructed to keep Him in our peripheral view. No, we are told to fix our eyes on Him.

To focus intently. To stare. To remain vigilant.

And the key to fixing your eyes on something is this: you can't fix your eyes on anything else.

If all we want is to be married, have a child, establish a career, be healed, reach a financial status or achieve a certain measure of power or control, then we are fixing our eyes on *that*. Not Him. And here is the same sobering thought in reverse: if we *don't* fix our eyes on Jesus, we will focus our attention elsewhere. It is human nature.

But not only are we to be proactive in running our race with Jesus at the helm, we must also be reactive to whatever interferes with that.

Verse one commands us to "throw off everything that hinders and the sin that so easily entangles." We are familiar with sin.

We understand the struggle. When we get tangled up in sinful behavior, we naturally end up heading in the wrong direction—in a direction opposite from Jesus. We understand the second half of that verse.

It is the first half that is not as well defined.

What are the things that hinder us? The word *hinder* comes from the Greek word *ogkos* which means "burden, weight, or encumbrance." It is the baggage we carry in our hearts. It is the parts of our lives that slow our race down or nudge us to veer off. And this extra weight is not necessarily sin—which is a careful distinction worth making. It is simply something that is diverting our attention from the task at hand.

A fixation may or may not be a sin, but it definitely hinders our race and needs to be thrown off.

When we fixate on anything other than Him, we become self-absorbed. We become hyper-focused on what we want or what we are lacking. We lose perspective and miss out on what we do have and what we aren't lacking. As a result, our destination becomes disappointment.

And that only fuels a greater fixation.

The hindrance I needed to throw off was my career expectations. The blueprints I had drawn up for myself were not sinful, but my intense desire for them slowly sent me in a direction that was outside of the boundary lines for my race. And that led to discouragement and a lack of contentment.

Everything that hinders is anything that causes us to take our eyes off of Jesus. It is anything that drives us to put ourselves first and says, "I am in charge of my life." It is whatever motivates a follower of Jesus to say, "I will not choose to follow you in that one area because what I want to do is more important." Or perhaps, it is the missed invitation to join Him in a greater work because we are only concerned with what we want. It is anything that deviates from the race. Anything that supersedes our agenda over His. Anything that causes us to forget that we are partnering with Him in this life, that He is in charge, and that He is worth following.

If we are fixated on anything other than Him, it needs to be thrown off.

Easier said than done, right?

Is something hindering you that needs to be thrown off? Pull out the mental blueprint you have drawn of your life and examine your longings. Start by asking yourself why you want them. Or what you hope to see happen. The answer may reveal itself immediately, or it might take some time to bubble up to the surface of your mind. But sit with it. Your answer might surprise you.

Be prepared for your longing to be a deeper, more basic yearning within you. It could be the need to be in control or the ache to be loved, or something to combat an insecurity. Maybe, like me, it could be an expectation you have or an unrealistic expectation you need to surrender. It is truly astounding how we can be motivated by something we are not consciously aware of. Don't discount the power of a deep need.

A greater understanding of what is truly yearning within you will help you answer the next question: Is this a desire or a fixation? There is a difference between wanting something and longing for it with such intensity that it consumes your thoughts. Use the following questions to help you further understand what lies within your heart. Mark the ones that resonate with you and spend some time journaling your answers.

What are you waiting for, and how intensely do you long for it? Are you fixated on it? How do you know that?

How focused are you on Jesus? In what ways are you running your race with Him as the prize? How are your eyes and attention fixed on Him?

Is there a sin(s) that has wound itself around you, slowing you down or leading you in a different direction? Spend time in Psalm 139:23-24 and 1 John 1:9 identifying and getting rid of it. Remember, sin is never your friend. Repentance is a gift. Embrace it.

What do you need to throw off in order to set your mind squarely on Him? Is something hindering you, weighing you down, or becoming a burden?

As you ponder and process these questions, invite some trusted friends into your circle. Ask for their thoughts, knowing wise words sometimes cut to the core, but when they are done in love, they reunite us to God in such profound ways. They snap us back to the right reality of who He is and who we are in Him. They expose our blind spots and cheer us on as we keep running our race.

Have I mentioned that friends like this are priceless?

Don't let the culture feed your fixation. If you are a follower of Christ, your life belongs to Him. You are not entitled to anything in this life. But you are promised abundant life! God has good plans for you. It may not be the plans that you have drawn up for yourself, but they are what God has tailor-made for you. That is the beauty of your partnership with Him.

We can't usher anything in or out of our external circumstances. We cannot force change. All we can do is ensure our gaze is firmly fixed on Jesus and trust Him to show us the next step.

In the next chapter, we will discuss an effective way to combat the culture and our inward drive to get what we want. But for now, lay your blueprint aside. Jesus wants to use your empty hands to fill them—not with a blueprint—but with a map.

You have a race to run with a precious prize awaiting. So, throw off everything that hinders.

He is worth it.

Lord, I surrender my fixation. Will you help me understand it? What is at the core of my desire? Do I have any hidden motivations? Is there a weight I need to throw off or a sin I need to confess and repent of? Give me insight to understand myself so I can loosen my grip and trust you with the boundary lines you have set for me. Help me hear your voice and follow your lead. Amen

Chapter Eight
The Benefits of Surrender

I distinctly remember the summer I turned 27. I had only one thing on my mind: getting married. The problem was I had not been on a date in four years. I was very single and there were no prospects in sight.

I had a rack of bridesmaid dresses in my closet and lots of random serving utensils I had accumulated over the years from throwing bridal showers. And that summer, I had started the next round of showers. Baby showers.

God help me.

I had gradually begun to struggle with singleness as each calendar year ticked by, but I was also busy working as a college minister and confident a wedding would be in my future. One day. Some day. Surely, I would be married by 27, right?

So, when that birthday drew near, I felt panic rising in my chest.

Ok, God. Where is he?

This isn't funny anymore.

You do have someone for me, don't you?

Don't you...?

Suddenly, my confidence began to wane, and my current circumstances took center stage. My circle of friends was either married, engaged, or dating. Things were not looking good. There were no such things as dating apps, and the online dating services available at that time were creepy. I was all by myself, waiting for God to bring me someone. The uncertainty was unnerving.

I knew if I wanted peace, it would have to come from God. I couldn't muster it up on my own. So, I decided to take a personal retreat. I booked a hotel for a few nights near a beautiful lake and hiking area and intentionally withdrew to be with God. I read and journaled and prayed and worshiped. I sat by the lake, hiked the trails, watched the sunset, and took long drives. I wrestled with my thoughts and desires and poured my heart out to God. At the end of my retreat, I wrote God a letter in my journal.

I told Him Scripture was clear that He loved me and that He was trustworthy. He was a good God and had good plans for me. I loved being in ministry and told Him as long as He kept using me, I would trust Him with the rest. I wanted to be married, but I wanted His will for me even more.

My heart was full as I penned the letter. I had spent quality time with Him and was basking in my renewed faith. I was acutely aware of His past faithfulness and walked confidently to my car to return home. I was grateful for the experience and easily slipped back into my normal routine. My future was in His hands, and I was at peace.

Well, that peace lasted for about two and a half weeks.

Then, without much triggering, the desire to be married came surging back. *Just kidding, God, I really want a husband.*

Since my dating life had not changed much in two and a half weeks, I knew I had a choice to make: be sad and scared of singleness or grab hold of His peace again. This time I didn't need a three-day retreat to help me. I just pulled out the letter I had written to God, reread it, recommitted to it, and then, without much fanfare, the peace returned.

This time my matrimonial desire stayed at bay for only a day or so. It was then that I realized I would need to seek peace on the regular if I wanted my heart to be at rest. I didn't like singleness staring me in the face every day, taunting me with fear and uncertainty. I knew God had more for me, and I didn't want this longing to hinder me from that. So, I began a little ritual. Every morning, I would roll out of bed right onto my knees and pray this simple prayer:

God, will you please give me a husband? That is my heart's desire. But for today, I am going to lay that desire down and choose to trust you with being single. You have this day planned for me, so please make it count. Use me today.

When I first started this roll-out-of-bed-into-prayer routine, I thought God would love my determination and possibly be impressed with my posture. I quietly assumed the repetition would work in my favor. But days turned into weeks that turned into months, and my single status remained just that, single.

Not. Even. One. Date.

Don't forget, though, that this simple prayer was actually two prayers. God had not budged on answering the first one. There were no men in my life. But almost immediately, I noticed His abundance in answering the second one: He was making my days count.

That year was the most fruitful year of ministry I had ever had. The college ministry where I worked was growing, and God was doing amazing things in and among these students. It was a privilege to be a part of their lives. And it was so easy to recognize that God was at work. He was blessing my morning ritual and using me to make a difference.

Now, I mentioned God had not budged on the first part of that prayer. My social life had not changed. Therefore, it appeared as if God was silent on the subject. But He wasn't. Rather, He was patiently teaching me a very valuable lesson. Through our partnership, He was forging in me a practice I would use over and over again for years to come.

He taught me what to do with my emotions.

Varying degrees of fear, sadness, disappointment, and jealousy greeted me like early morning birds. They were chirping and flitting about all around my mind. This prayer helped me scoop them up and entrust them to God's safekeeping. I didn't stuff them down, try to hide them, or pretend they weren't there. Instead, I acknowledged my emotions and then did something with them. Every morning, I put my desire to be married and the emotions that came with that into His hands and let go. In other words, I surrendered it to Him.

It wasn't until after I had laid everything down that I could focus on the day ahead. Once my emotions were not front and center in my mind, I could direct myself to move forward with joyful anticipation. I was expecting good things because good things were happening.

As time ticked on, my heart became accustomed to the peace that was available to me every morning. And I loved how God was using me at work! I completed both the fall and the spring semesters without a single date under my belt, but with a heart full of joy and peace. Did I still want to be married? Yes. But did it consume me like it did before? No.

I wanted it, but I was learning I would be okay without it. Being a part of how God was working in the lives of those around me was fully satisfying, and I knew if that continued, my life would still be full and meaningful.

This little prayer time was super effective in my life, but it wasn't my idea. Rather, the secret to my contentment was found in the form of an instruction written centuries ago and recorded in the Book of Hebrews.

When we become fixated on our longings, our emotions take charge. The act of zeroing in on what we want can run so deep, it is hard to break free from the cycle it creates. We need a new strategy to counteract this forged pathway in our hearts and minds. But knowing we need to replace or redirect our emotions can feel next to impossible.

When Waiting Feels Like Withholding

How do we lay aside what we long for the most? It can feel insurmountable.

Thankfully, God's Word is clear, effective, and accessible for our use. In Hebrews 4, we find a verse loaded with spiritual gems.

"Let us then approach God's throne of grace with confidence, so that we may receive mercy and find grace to help us in our time of need" (v. 16).

There are several things worth noting in this verse. First, we are invited to approach God. How wonderful is that? It is easy to skim past it, forgetting that we are not only encouraged to draw near to Him, but we are enabled to do so! Sin no longer separates us from God. We can approach Him and come into His presence! Don't rush past the fact that Jesus paid a high price so we could freely enter into God's presence.

The second part worth noting is that when we approach God, we can do so with confidence. What does that mean? It means we can draw near to Him, knowing He will welcome us, receive us, and hear us. We can hold our heads high knowing we are loved and precious in His sight. There are no fears involved. It means we can bring our requests before Him—confidently!

Next, according to this verse, what happens when we approach Him with confidence? We receive mercy. We find grace. He helps us when we are in need. Who does not want that? What a theologically rich verse!

But we are not done yet.

Like any part of Scripture, we must read this verse in its entirety. And there is a tiny word in it that we tend to overlook—a word that puts all the other words in their proper context. And understanding the Bible in its proper context is key to living it out effectively.

Glance back at the verse on the previous page and circle what we are approaching.

We are approaching a throne.

We can't forget who God is and what His role is in our lives. We can approach God with confidence, knowing He wants to extend mercy and grace in our time of need. But don't miss the fact that we are approaching Him on His throne. We are approaching Him with respect and reverence. We are approaching Him, through our partnership with Him, as our Lord.

Jesus came before His Father's throne in the Garden of Gethsemane. The night before His crucifixion, He approached God with confidence. He poured out His heart saying, "My Father, if it be possible, let this cup pass from me; nevertheless, not as I will, but as you will" (Matthew 26:39). Jesus clearly asked for what He wanted, but with no demands. He put His request out there, acknowledging that He would accept whatever God decided.

Notice how the word "throne" puts the word "approach" in context. That one word says a lot! You will move toward someone on a throne much differently than someone sitting on a beanbag chair. This descriptor shows you how to approach.

It also further defines the word "confidence." As you envision God on His throne, you can't help but be reminded of His power and magnitude. And what a picture of the intimate nature of our relationship with Him. We can boldly ask for what we want! We can draw near to Him with assurance and courage. The word "confidence" is richly and deeply defined when described through the lens of a throne.

This one word also puts the mercy and grace we are going to receive into context. These are not flippant words we throw around. Mercy and grace are freely given and terribly undeserved. Only someone who is Lord over our lives can extend them to us.

As you can see, understanding the significance of the word "throne" puts this entire act of prayer in context. If we don't understand this word, we don't understand this verse.

So, yes, approach Him with confidence; ask boldly for what you want! But do so with the reverence and respect that is due Him. Remember whom you are approaching. Following in the footsteps of Jesus, you can pray something like this:

Lord, can I please have _____?
Though not my will, but yours be done.

Do you see the mixture of confidence and reverence? Because He is your loving Heavenly Father, share your deepest desires with Him! Hold them out there for Him to see. But then lay them down at His feet. Let Him have the final say. Trust His direction in your life. This is the heart of our partnership with Him.

It is all about the act of letting go. The act of surrendering. And with surrender comes a hidden blessing.

In 1 Samuel 1, we find Hannah at a very low point in life. She desperately wanted a child, and year after year her womb was empty. To make matters worse, her husband had another wife who was very fruitful.

And spiteful.

And rude.

Scripture tells us Elkanah loved his wife Hannah more than his other wife. And I am betting wife number two wasn't a fan of that, so she regularly reminded Hannah of her inability to conceive.

When Waiting Feels Like Withholding

One day during a meal, Hannah was in tears from her rival's vicious comments and her own sadness. She was unable to eat. But at some point, she wiped her tears and stood up. She made the decision to leave the dinner table and go pray. She approached God with confidence and poured out her heart to Him. With fresh tears, she wept bitterly and begged Him for a child.

And then something interesting happened.

Verse 18 tells us, "...then she went her way and ate something, and her face was no longer downcast." How was she able to eat again? Why was her face no longer downcast? What happened while she prayed?

The answer is simple: Hannah surrendered.

She took her desire and all the emotions swirling around it and laid them down. She surrendered her longing to God, and once she did, she was able to get up and eat. Her face reflected that her heart had stopped grieving bitterly. Now, would the ache for motherhood return?

Maybe.

Probably.

But in that moment, she had peace.

While surrendering has a lot of negative connotations, it doesn't mean "no." Nor is it an automatic assumption that your dream or longing will go unfulfilled. True surrender is simply the decision to release something so that it won't develop a hold on you, causing you to assume you cannot survive without it. Failure to surrender can slowly deplete your joy, satisfaction, and contentment. For Hannah, her longing for a baby had a tight grip on her soul, draining the life out of her. But after she prayed and surrendered, the grip was released.

Scripture tells us Hannah went on to conceive and give birth to Samuel. But that is not the point. The point is, she found peace in the midst of her waiting. Before she showed any signs of pregnancy, she was at rest in her heart.

Peace doesn't come from the desired answer to prayer. It comes through surrender.

Surrender is the only thing that can prevent our emotions from taking charge. It keeps the desire from strangling your heart and allows you to breathe deeply. While it may appear hard to do at first, the freedom it produces is worth it. Surrender is an act that returns to us as a gift. It is the beautiful benefit of partnering with someone who loves us and has our best interest in mind.

Let's talk about how to do this on a practical level.

A simple way to remember Hebrews 4:16 is by using your fist as an analogy. What do we do with the longings we have? We reach for them and grab hold of them! We grip them tightly in our hands and don't let go, right? Let's take this seizing and clutching response and apply this verse to it.

Imagine whatever you long for is nestled securely in your fist. Your fingers are tightly wrapped around it. Now, follow the next two steps.

First, approach God with confidence. Extend your fist outward a little and crack open your fingers to form a bowl with your hand. Tell God what is inside. Confidently ask Him for what you have in your palm.

Next, remember you are approaching His throne. Fully extend your arm and spread wide your fingers. Allow the desire to roll out of your hand, leaving your hand empty. Trust God to hold your desire for you and do with it what He deems best.

The first step is usually our natural response in prayer. We loosen our grip just enough for God to be able to peek and see what lies inside. We point at it and hold it up for Him to see, but we don't let go of it. We simply show it to Him.

We can't stop there, though. Because we are approaching God on His throne, we must extend our arms and spread our fingers wide, fully releasing our desires to Him. We engage in the act of surrender. And do you know what God's response to us is? He gently takes the dream from our hands and holds it with as much care as we did. He doesn't toss it aside absentmindedly or tear it up nonchalantly. He doesn't flippantly throw away a desire we have surrendered or stuff it in a pocket to be soon forgotten. No, He considers the weight of it and holds it with appropriate care. He knows we have trusted Him with something significant, and He responds with the same level of sincerity.

Complete surrender is key to this process, though. If all we do is approach Him with confidence and boldly make our requests, we are hindering the work of God in our lives. Ironically, the tighter we hold on to something, the harder it is for God to work the issue out in us. So why do we keep holding on? Because we fear what comes next. Consider the fist analogy again. After you spread wide your fingers to Him, what are you left with?

An empty hand.

Yuck. An empty hand feels, well, empty. Lonely. Lacking. Deprived. Wanting. Suddenly, you regret letting go of your desire. The emptiness in return can sometimes feel worse than the longing. That is why we grip our dreams so tightly. But can I help you reframe this empty hand? Let's look at it differently.

An empty hand is an open hand.

Once your hand is open, God can fill it.

He might fill it with what you want, but He might give you something different. Something unexpected. Something you never thought you needed. True surrender results in His peace, rest, and emotional reprieve.

With an open hand, you are now in the posture to receive.

I am guessing that by this point in the book you know I have a husband. After a year of praying for one, I began dating Dave. A few months after we got married, I was unpacking boxes in our new apartment and came across the journal from that personal retreat I took when I was 27. I was suddenly curious to reread the letter I had written to God. I quickly flipped through it until I found the entry from my three-day experience. I gasped as I stared at the page. The day I had penned this letter to God was July 20, and my wedding day, two years later, was July 20. I had no idea they were on the same day until that moment.

When I allowed God to take that desire from my hand, He held it with care. He never dropped it or forgot about it. Instead, my empty hand was now an open hand that He could fill. For a year, I opened my hand to Him each morning, allowing Him to put what I needed most in it. He filled it with a fruitful ministry and later a husband. He also filled it with peace, the ability to trust Him, and rest from the emotional barrage of singleness. But, most importantly, He filled it with the experiential knowledge of the power and goodness of surrender.

And that was the true treasure.

Learning to surrender, continually trust, and receive from God (whatever it might be!) are invaluable lessons. I did gain a husband, but I also gained so much more. I learned what to do with my longings. I learned I could trust Him to hold them for me. I learned that no matter what He filled my open hand with; I was going to be okay. Surrender is not a guarantee that you will receive what you are relinquishing. But it is a guarantee that you will find peace and rest for your soul.

The weight of our emotions can be unbearable at times. Our motivations, fixations, and expectations can cloud our ability to discern what's best. But it has never been our job to discern what's best. That is God's job. So, when we surrender, we pass the reins back to Him and let Him lead.

There is freedom in surrender.

Consider your hands today. Where do your desires lie? In a tightly closed fist, peeking out from your palm, or resting in God's hands?

Pour out your heart. Aim for surrender. Embrace His peace.

Chapter Nine
Battling Fear

I collapse in the face of fear. It is the fastest and easiest way to bring me down, and the enemy knows it. I often resemble the Israelites who boldly marched out of Egypt after the tenth plague (Exodus 14:8), only to crumble like stale cake two verses later at the sight of their enemies who were in fast pursuit. My heart can deflate in an instant when faced with a scary situation.

But I know I am not alone.

Fear is just as rampant in the Scriptures as it is in our daily lives. All throughout the tissue pages of my Bible are stories of real people dealing with real problems. Problems that are fraught with angst. Alarming scenarios that keep us on the edge of *our* seats. So, good news! We are not alone. The bad news, however, is that fear isn't going anywhere. It is an effective tactic, so the enemy keeps it handy.

We haven't mentioned the devil much in this book, but he is alive and well in the in-between. Why? Because seasons of waiting can move us into vulnerable spaces. They can elevate our insecurities as well as make us hypersensitive. The enemy will not hesitate to pounce on us when we are operating on less than all cylinders. He loves to kick us while we are down. And fear is such an easy way to do that.

There is often a low hum of anxiety playing in the soundtrack of our minds as we wait on God. And it doesn't take much for that hum to escalate into a blaring horn. We can't help but wonder how our situations will play out. What are our relationships, finances, family dynamics, and dreams going to look like in the end? When we are intimately acquainted with uncertainty, ambiguity, and the unknown, we often find fear lurking nearby.

So how do we temper fear and find peace amidst the uncertainty of waiting?

Just about any story you read involving the Israelites includes fear. They were known for wobbly knees and trembling hearts. Sometimes they would surge ahead with confidence, but eventually they would circle back to biting their nails and wringing their hands with worry.

It is so easy to look at the nation of Israel and shake our heads. Why couldn't they learn from their mistakes and trust God? The relentless cycle of ups and downs is exhausting. But in my honest moments, I know I am more like the Israelites than I care to admit. I can be running my race with incredible faith and profound courage only to be halted in my tracks by one person's actions or one fleeting thought. Fear is a relentless cycle in my life too.

And like the Israelites, my fears start out the same way.

Consider the classic example found in Numbers 13. The Israelites had just escaped from Egypt when we find them trudging through the desert en route to the Promised Land. When they arrive at the border, Moses charges 12 men to enter the land and report back their findings. Joshua and Caleb famously returned confident, but the other ten were teetering on the edge of panic.

"The people who live there are powerful, and the cities are fortified and very large," they announced (v. 28). In addition, they cried, "We can't attack those people; they are stronger than we are" (v. 31). Finally, as an exclamation point to their report they said, "The land we explored *devours* those living in it" (v. 32, emphasis mine).

Their account sent the rest of the Israelites into hysterics, and they bemoaned their escape from Egypt, begging to return. Fear had the Israelites by the throat, and their faith was quickly squeezed out.

I can't help but laugh at the fact that God called their destination the "Promised Land." It wasn't the You-Might-Get-It Land, or the I-Hope-You-Get-It Land or the You-Better-Be-Strong-Enough Land. No, it was the Promised Land. The land was promised to them. God's choice of words should have instilled confidence, but it didn't. Why?

In order to answer that, we need to understand more about fear.

Fear knows how to become front and center in our minds. It is a fairly simple technique. So simple that we easily miss it. Are you ready for it?

Fear creates a future scenario that does not include the presence of God.

A wise friend once told me anxiety is often in the future. Rarely in the present. Our worries lie in what has not yet happened. They are assumptions that paint pictures of doom and destruction. They are scenarios that we are terrified will become realities.

If fear can get us to imagine a situation where God is absent or not in control, we are left paralyzed to move forward. In addition to that, fear's nature is to give us spiritual amnesia. As it wipes Him from our future, it simultaneously wipes Him from our past. We suddenly forget the majesty and magnificence of our very *mighty* Father.

Consider the Israelites. They just witnessed God miraculously rescuing them from Egypt. They watched the ten plagues unfold and pave the way for their mass exodus. They experienced the Red Sea parting before their eyes, allowing them to cross over unharmed. They stood in awe as the sea collapsed in on itself again, destroying the entire Egyptian army. Make no mistake, they had seen the power of God. But now, a few short weeks later, they spy on the land God had *promised* to them and return with nothing but fear.

Look back at their descriptions of the city and the people. They stated they were powerful, fortified, large, and strong. Can you see the scene they were creating in their minds? They were picturing themselves fighting against these mighty warriors. But where was God?

As the story goes, after the ten spies sufficiently terrified the Israelites, the nation went into hysterics. But Joshua and Caleb were different. They were the voice of opposition. The voice of faith. They tore their clothes and begged the people to listen to them.

"Do not be afraid of the people of the land, because we will devour them. Their protection is gone, but the Lord is with us. Do not be afraid of them" (Numbers 14:9).

Did you catch that? What reason did Joshua and Caleb provide as to why they should not be afraid?

"Their protection is gone, but the Lord is with us."

Did the Amalekites, Hittites, Jebusites, and Amorites suddenly lose their weapons? Did the fortified cities somehow crumble? Did these men shrink and no longer tower over them? No. Those outward circumstances had not changed. The difference between Joshua and Caleb and the other ten spies was they pictured God going to battle with them. They had their mighty Father in mind as they imagined the fighting that would ensue.

They remembered when the frogs swept through the land and the Egyptians panicked. (Exodus 8)

They remembered the cries of the Egyptians when their firstborn children were found dead. (Exodus 12)

They remembered the Egyptian army closing in on them and the Red Sea beginning to part. (Exodus 14)

They remembered the moment the sea came crashing down on their enemies. (Exodus 14)

They remembered the next morning when they sang a song of victory. (Exodus 15)

God was with them when they fled from Egypt, and God would be with them when they entered the Promised Land. God was not absent in their future scenario. He was very much a part of the picture, and as a result, Joshua and Caleb knew their enemy's protection was gone. Their enemies did not stand a chance against their God. It was as if they didn't even have any weapons!

Do you see how simple this is? For the devil and for us? If Satan can get you to remove God from the equation in your mind, then he automatically has a leg up. How quickly we spiral out of control when we fail to include the presence of God in our future scenarios. The enemy is no match for God. He is embarrassingly miniscule in comparison.

And Satan knows that.

So, because he can't go toe to toe with God, he knows his only option is to remove Him. And since he can't actually remove Him, he aims to pretend. The only battle Satan can win is in the mind. And the only way he can win that battle is if God is absent from it. The enemy can never defeat the presence of God in any situation—real life or imagined.

So all we have to do is make sure He is present in our minds? That seems so simple—too simple. Right?

But try it.

What is something you are deeply worried about today? What scenarios are you fearful will become a reality? Will the doctor deliver bad news? Will your child continue in a life of destruction? Will you lose that job? Will you never get married or have a child? Examine your thoughts and the way your future scenario plays out. Is God sitting with you when the doctor is talking? Is He walking beside your child into dark places? Is He lying with you at night and greeting you with courage in the morning?

We can easily turn the tide and restore our courage by simply painting Him back into the picture. Or by never removing Him to begin with!

I remember the first time I applied this simple principle in my life. I was a senior in college, and my local church had asked me to share my testimony at a Sunday evening event. I had never done that before, and I was a nervous wreck. I still remember what I wore that night—an off-white pantsuit with matching off-white pumps. I had on gold earrings and a simple necklace with a gold cross. But what I remember even more about that night was sitting in my car in the parking lot, afraid to go inside. I recall putting my head on the steering wheel and praying, "God, please go with me into that church." Instantly this verse popped into my head:

"…I am with you always, to the very end of the age" (Matthew 28:20).

In that moment, I knew He was with me. I got out of my car, and as I walked across the parking lot, I pictured Jesus with me. As I sat in the church pew waiting for my turn in the program, I imagined Him sitting next to me. And as I walked up the few short steps to the podium, I could feel courage welling up inside me. I could stand and tell this crowd my story because He was doing it with me.

I don't remember anything after I shared it, but I'm sure I told my story and was back in my seat a few minutes later. The rest of the evening was unmemorable, but the lesson I learned that night was not. Jesus never left my side that evening. So, if I can imagine Him with me in the moment, why can't I imagine Him with me in my future? At what point will He ever not be there?

Don't forget the reason the Israelites spent 40 years in the desert was because of their moment of panic with the ten spies. Their inability to include God in their mind's eye cost them dearly. But what about the rest of the story? Let's fast forward four decades.

After all those years, the Israelites are finally on the brink of entering the Promised Land. But unfortunately, they are still fearful. This time, however, God graciously paints the future for them. Look how Moses describes their pending entrance into the land, now 40 years later:

"Be strong and courageous. Do not be afraid or terrified because of them, for the Lord your God goes with you; he will never leave you nor forsake you" (Deuteronomy 31:6).

Moses didn't tell them there would be nothing to fear. He didn't chastise them for being fearful. Going into battle is no small feat! He simply pinpointed the one thing they did not need to be afraid of: their enemies.

And it is worth noting that the strategy for battling fear never changed. God didn't give Moses different instructions for their second attempt. Joshua and Caleb's courage was directly linked to their confidence in God's presence going with them. And now, 40 years later, Moses was reminding them to do the very same thing.

It is so easy to picture the battle as us versus them. Us versus the unfulfilled dream, the diagnosis, the financial strain, the disappointing relationship. But instead, let's picture it as us *and God* versus them.

Doesn't the difference between those two statements instill courage in you? Knowing God is with us is huge.

When your imagination starts to run wild, look around. Do you see God? Is He part of the scenario or inconspicuously absent? Take note when you don't find Him there, knowing it can be quickly remedied.

The apostle Paul supports this claim in

Romans 8. He states, "I am convinced... that neither present nor future... can separate us from the love of God that is in Christ Jesus our Lord" (vv. 38-39). And since God is love (1 John 4:8), then nothing in the future can separate us from God.

We cannot create a scenario that God is unable to be a part of.

Unless we choose to.

Fear is a natural response to prolonged periods of waiting. But God knows that. He is not asking us to stop allowing fear to creep in. He is not shaking His head in disgust because, once again, we are afraid. He knows fear is inevitable. Instead, He knows if we want to battle it, we have to replace it. We can't just ball up our fists and will fear away from our minds. We have to switch it out to get rid of it. So, He provides the perfect swap.

Himself.

Fear has no power over us as long as we keep our Heavenly Father in the center of our circumstances. His presence is all we need. And though it might seem simple, the key to unlocking that power is to visualize Him in your situation with you.

Involve Him in that hard conversation.

Picture Him walking with you into that stressful situation.

Know He is sitting next to you as you grieve.

Use His past faithfulness to strengthen your visualization. Remember His power, provision, and protection, and allow that to steady you and instill confidence in you. "Jesus is the same yesterday, today, and tomorrow" (Hebrews 13:8). If He was present in your past, you can count on Him in your future.

God is not absent, weak, or unaware. So don't picture Him as such. Think of Him as Scripture depicts Him and place Him in the center of your story. Let His omnipresence comfort your soul and give you rest.

Your season of waiting does not have to be marked by or ruled by fear. Peace is available to you through the presence of God. So, combat your worry with that promise.

You are not alone, dear one, because you cannot be alone. And don't let fear tell you otherwise!

> "When you pass through the waters, I will be with you. When you pass through the rivers, they will not sweep over you.
>
> When you walk through the fire you will not be burned; the flames will not set you ablaze.
>
> For I am the Lord your God, the Holy One of Israel, your Savior" (Isaiah 43:2-3).

Chapter Ten
The Secret to Perseverance

When my older son was four, he examined the broccoli on his plate and announced that he "just couldn't eat it." To emphasize his point, he gently placed his hand on the small of his back, slightly winced, and explained it made his back hurt.

Disclaimer: As I metioned in chapter 1, I began dealing with chronic back pain around the time of my child-rearing years. It was commonplace to see me hunched over, limping, or lying down. My son had learned that spinal issues earned you privileges in life (lots of lying down and people waiting on you), and he thought that might translate into vegetables. As he looked at his dinner plate, he skillfully mimicked the way I put my hand on my back when I was hurting. I had to smile at his effort.

As ridiculous as his reasoning was, his sincerity was heartfelt. At the core of his being, he was convinced that that particular floret could not be swallowed. As a parent, I knew otherwise.

I think that's how God feels when we reach a breaking point—when waiting takes a toll, and we decide enough is enough. We just can't do it anymore. Maybe we hit a wall due to the length of time that has passed or the intensity of the experience. It could be a myriad of other compelling reasons too. We aren't strong enough or smart enough. We have too much anger and / or sadness. The list goes on. The point is, we decide the issue is too big. We are done.

Yet God knows otherwise. Unlike an unpopular vegetable conversation, He isn't tickled on the inside by our reasoning. Rather, He agrees with us.

Yes, this is big.

Yes, this is hard.

You are lacking.

You *will* need more.

And that "more" is tucked away in a not-so-popular passage in the New Testament.

The Book of James doesn't mince words. The author starts off strong with a clear, albeit challenging, view of suffering.

"Consider it pure joy whenever you face

When Waiting Feels Like Withholding

trials of many kinds, because you know that the testing of your faith produces perseverance. Let perseverance finish its work so you may be mature and complete, not lacking anything" (James 1:2-4).

At first glance, verse two can read that we should be happy about trials—that we should welcome difficulty and look hardship in the eye with praise. But that is not correct. Rather, it says we should consider it joy (pure joy, to be exact!) when you *face* trials. Now, that might not seem like a difference big enough to get excited about. I understand that. Anytime joy and trials are in the same sentence, we are leery to accept it. But we must look at the end of the passage to appreciate the clarity of the beginning of it.

According to verse four, trials lead to maturity. Trials bring completion and help us not to lack anything. Therefore, we can be joyful about facing a trial because we know what the trial will produce in us.

Here's my paraphrase of this: Consider it pure joy when you get the opportunity to trust Jesus with a trial, knowing it will make you mature, complete, and not lacking anything.

We don't take joy in the trial, but in the opportunity to trust Him with it.

Now let me be crystal clear: We are not required to be happy about suffering. We are allowed to and expected to cry, grieve, get angry, etc. as we journey through difficulty. We do not have to love the trial or the process of the trial. The only thing to love is the promise that Jesus will see us through it and make us stronger as a result.

Don't rush past that!

Jesus never tells us to fend for ourselves when experiencing a trial. Nor is there a trial so devastating that God cannot bring good from it. Every challenge we face gives us the opportunity to trust Jesus and, when we do, we can be certain He will carry us through to the end, making us more mature and complete in the process.

On paper, this looks good. Hard times equal maturity. It is easy to get on board with that, right? So what is the catch? We don't jump from trials to maturity in an instant. What is the bridge connecting them? The bridge is the "P" word tucked in between these two verses.

Perseverance.

I know the knee-jerk response to that word is to sigh. It just feels hard to accept, doesn't it? Perseverance conjures up a slew of unpleasant words in my mind: effort, not giving up, sweat, patience, hard work, weariness, discipline, etc. But according to this verse, it is viewed in a very positive light. James appears a bit giddy that a trial will produce perseverance. In his mind, perseverance is a good thing because it leads to maturity. It is the necessary stepping-stone to our ultimate goal.

Paul, in Romans 5, also speaks well of this word.

"Not only so, but we also glory in our sufferings, because we know that suffering produces perseverance; perseverance, character; and character, hope" (vv. 3-4).

James 1 and Romans 5 both paint a beautiful picture of what perseverance produces in us. If someone asked you if you wanted character, hope, maturity, completion, and not to be lacking anything, what would you say?

Enough said.

According to both New Testament authors, however, perseverance doesn't happen on its own. It must be preceded by trials and suffering. So though we go to enormous lengths to avoid any kind of discomfort, we can take heart knowing our pain will never be in vain. God uses it to produce things in us that cannot be produced any other way.

If you have made it this far in the book, I assume you have dealt with trials and suffering. You are in the midst of something you would rather not be dealing with. If so, the good news is you have activated perseverance. You have kick-started the key ingredient necessary for character, hope, maturity, and completion. Oh, and you are on your way to not lacking anything either.

Remember the "more" I said we would need at the beginning of this chapter? The thing we need when we hit the wall and say we can't do it anymore? This is it. Perseverance is the "more."

Perseverance looks different depending on your situation. No two journeys are exactly the same. But there are some core characteristics that each of us will experience, so let's take a closer look at the definition of perseverance and what it looks like in the life of a follower of Christ. It is worth noting that perseverance has unique aspects that set it apart from simply pressing on in life. And to experience the good results as described in Scripture, we must commit to walk in perseverance through a biblical lens.

So, what does perseverance look like for a follower of Christ? Consider this very basic description:

Perseverance plays out in what you believe and how you act. In your heart you trust God, and, in your actions you honor Him. Both need to line up. You may not like your situation, but you trust He is in it, and you let integrity and conviction lead you through it.

Eugene Peterson famously authored the book *A Long Obedience In The Same*

Direction. It was written over 40 years ago, and though the premise of the book is about the Christian life in general, I think it can be applied in specific settings, too.

Perseverance is a long obedience in the same direction—a long obedience of trust. Trusting that God sees you, understands your situation, is guiding you through it, and is good. Of course, that doesn't mean you feel fully convinced of all these things every day. But you are aiming for trust. You are asking for it. You are wrestling with God in order to get to that place.

Perseverance is striving to tell God you trust Him and that you will continue to follow Him no matter what.

That might mean taking time every day to pray for that child who is hurting or struggling even when you don't see change. It might mean showing up for the counseling appointment and choosing to be vulnerable, knowing your spouse may not. It could be choosing to believe God will take care of you, even when the financial strain still exists. It could be accepting your current stage in life despite your ache to be married, to be a parent, or to accomplish a goal.

Persevering is saying, "yes" to a day you would rather say, "no" to, trusting that God has not forgotten you and is fully in control of the situation. It is believing He is good despite an array of bad circumstances.

Trusting means choosing to spend time with Him, reading His Word, understanding it, and choosing to live by it.

The reason why perseverance is so hard is because we get overwhelmed with the duration of it. The thought of repeatedly saying, "yes" to a day I want to say, "no" to, can be unbearable. So let me share some good news with you, a little secret about perseverance.

You only have to persevere one day at a time.

You don't have to stare down the barrel of a trial and muster up enough perseverance for the entire trial, whether that be days, weeks, or even years. No. Your only responsibility is for today.

Persevere today.

Trust Him today.

Act with integrity today.

Make choices that honor Him today.

I can do anything for a day. It's imagining the thought of doing it for a week, a month, or a year that leaves me defeated. That kind of perseverance I can quickly grow weary of.

And for those trials that might remain permanent this side of heaven, this applies even more. It is in those lifelong battles that we must be reminded we only need to persevere one day at a time.

Currently, I'm in a trial that keeps morphing into more trials. Today, in fact, I received an email with more bad news. I immediately reminded myself I only had to persevere for today. I cried, told God how I felt, and then concentrated on the good things that are promised me in James 1:4. My prayer was simple:

I will trust you with this email, knowing you are in it, not surprised by it, and fully prepared to walk me through it. In trusting you with this, I will become more mature and complete. Thank you for that promise. Amen

Now I realize a painful email does not compare to a painful in-between. Waiting for God to restore a marriage, heal a disease, provide for desperate finances, or allow a woman to conceive feels much weightier than an email that made me feel less than and rejected. But hear me say this: the principle is the same.

Every day we trust God with our circumstances, we are taking one tiny step toward maturity. We may not be able to see the step. The change may be so incremental we don't even notice it. But it's there. And one tiny step followed by another tiny step means forward progress toward hope, character, and completion. Always.

And *that* we can consider pure joy!

On the days you think you "just can't do it anymore," ask yourself if you can do it for one day. Just today. There are so many verses in Scripture reminding us not to get ahead of ourselves. Jesus encourages us in Matthew 6 to "not worry about tomorrow because today has enough worries of its own" (v. 34). Solomon wisely reminds us in Proverbs 27:1, "do not boast about tomorrow, for you do not know what a day may bring." And don't forget how God dealt with the Israelites in the desert for 40 years. How often did the manna appear on the ground for them to eat? Every day and twice on the sixth day (so they could rest on the seventh day). Do you see how intentional God was? He wanted them to learn on a very practical level that He was going to show up every day. No exceptions. He could be trusted. Their needs were always going to be met.

Life is meant to be lived today. Tomorrow belongs to the Lord.

We often think of seizing the day and making the most of it when we are doing something fun or memorable. But what if we applied the same principle to perseverance? What if we only tried to persevere one day at a time?

Sit for a minute and consider your season of waiting. What would it feel like to trust God with it for one day? Cease thinking about tomorrow. Simply focus on today. How would your prayers change? Or your outlook on the situation? What about your stress level? How would you relate to others? Would anything else change? Consider setting aside some time to journal your thoughts on this. How could you remind yourself to persevere for one day at a time?

Trials will impact you. They can make you better or worse. But they will not leave you the same.

Join me in choosing better.

In choosing trust.

In persevering.

One day at a time.

Chapter Eleven
When God Says No

Margaret Feinberg, in her book Scouting the Divine, describes the heartbreaking scene of a hen waiting for her infertile eggs to hatch. She notes the hen is repeatedly walking in a circle and asks Lynn, the farmer, why. Lynn states the hen is looking for her eggs but that she had tossed the eggs into the creek earlier that day. Appalled, Margaret asks why. The farmer explains that the hen had been sitting on her eggs for three months, so obviously they were not going to hatch. But a hen will not stop brooding until the egg cracks open with life. So, the eggs must be removed for the hen to be able to move on. At first, the hen will circle the spot where the eggs used to be, but in time will return to the life she should be living. What seemed cruel at first, Margaret now understood to be kind and compassionate.

I remember the day I read that story. I had spent months praying about having another child. I wanted one, but my husband didn't. We each had a list of reasons why and were struggling to agree. I wanted what was best for our family and asked God to either change my heart or my husband's heart (though if I am honest, my prayers were heavily biased in my favor).

When I read that story, I felt God gently speak to my heart. *Stop going in circles, Jen.* I remember gasping out loud in my bed as I lay snuggled in my comforter, about to nod off. I wanted to unread the story, but I couldn't. I knew I was a hen going in circles and there were no more eggs to be found. God was using this visual image to show me my family was complete.

I had asked God for more children, and He said no. It took me several weeks to tell my husband what had happened that night. I knew once I said it out loud that it would be final in real life. So I needed time to accept it. But after a few weeks, I shared with him this story, and we settled the matter of our family's future.

Margaret's reflection on the farmer's decision to toss the eggs in the creek stuck with me:

"Lynn's answer helped me understand her

action as one of compassion and wisdom. I couldn't help but wonder how often I have sat on dreams that were never going to come to fruition or, worse, sat on the empty promises of the enemy that would never yield life—only self-destruction and death." [1]

When God says no, it is hard. Nothing rattles our understanding of God's love for us more than a "no." Everything about it is tough. In fact, I am betting this is the one chapter you didn't want to read. The title itself is unsettling. We don't like "no." But how can we discuss seasons of waiting and not talk about when He answers differently than we had hoped? If our in-between has been reduced to us repeatedly circling the ground in search of something that isn't there, don't we want to know it?

I am sure we do. But it is still hard. So let's talk about it.

What do we do when God says no?

There are clear examples of God saying no to people in both the Old Testament and the New Testament. Moses asks for permission to enter the Promised Land and is denied (Deuteronomy 3:26-28). David fasts and prays for his sick son, begging God to spare his life, and yet he dies (2 Samuel 12:15-18). A demon-possessed man is healed by Jesus and begs to travel with Him, but Jesus tells him to go home and tell everyone what God has done (Mark 5:18-20). Paul states that he has been given a "thorn in his flesh," and he pleads three times for the Lord to take it away. God said no (2 Corinthians 12:7-9).

At this point in our journey together, I think we know why God says no. Sometimes He is making room for something better, or to protect us from harm. In other instances, saying no furthers His mission to make Himself known or is in response to a sin in our lives. Sometimes, He is simply leading us to depend on Him by steering us away from what we are currently depending on. Each of the biblical characters mentioned above falls into one of these categories.

As we have already discussed, God's ways are higher than ours. We don't always understand Him. But we can trust He cares about us, has not forgotten us, and isn't punishing us. As we allow conviction—not condemnation—to speak to us, as we loosen our grip and surrender our desires, as we wrestle to keep fear at bay and aim to persevere one day at a time, we might reach the place where God says no. The place where we stop circling the eggs, hoping they will hatch.

And then what do we do?

I don't think we need further explanation of why God says no. Instead, we need to know what to do in response to it.

In the biblical stories of Moses, David, the demon-possessed man, and Paul, we see four different responses to God's denial of their requests. You probably are not going to like them. As I first thought about them, I immediately felt resistance in my heart. If I were to list my four responses to God saying no, they would be: disappointment, frustration, sorrow, and confusion. But thankfully, my heart and my stories are not memorialized in Scripture.

These men all responded to God differently. Are you ready for them? Deep breath.

Acceptance

Worship

Obedience

Delight

If walls have suddenly come up around your heart, that's okay. I understand. I don't like these responses any more than you do, so let's take a closer look and let the Scriptures describe these reactions. Then we can tackle the deeper issue:

How did these men respond this way?

A common thread weaves these men's stories together, and I would like to unravel it for us to see. But first, let's examine their responses.

Moses: Acceptance

During the Israelites' 40-year trek through the desert, the people grumbled to Moses to satisfy their thirst. In Numbers 20:8, God hears their cries and tells Moses to hold the staff and speak to the rock, commanding it to pour forth water. Instead, Moses takes the staff and strikes it on the rock. The rock produced water, but God was not happy with Moses' disobedience. He had wanted Moses to speak to the rock, not strike it.

That one action cost Moses his entrance into the Promised Land.

I know, I know. I struggle with this, too. It seems incredibly strict. Did it really matter if he struck the rock or spoke to it? Apparently, yes. God had issued a clear command, and Moses did not obey it. And according to God, that action compromised His holiness (Numbers 20:12).

So, what was Moses' reaction? We find our answer in the Book of Deuteronomy. This Old Testament book is Moses' farewell speech to the Israelites. It is a recap of their 40-year journey in the desert, reminding them what God had done and passing the leadership baton to Joshua. In chapter 3, Moses shares his plea with God:

"At that time, I pleaded with the Lord: 'Sovereign Lord, you have begun to show to your servant your greatness and your strong hand. For what god is there in heaven or on earth who can do the deeds and mighty works you do? Let me go over and see the good land beyond the Jordan—that fine hill country and Lebanon'" (Deuteronomy 3:23-25).

God remained resolute and denied the request (v.26). However, He did instruct Moses to climb atop Mount Pisgah and view the expanse of the land with his own eyes. So, after the speech is over, we see Moses do this:

"Then Moses climbed Mount Nebo from the plains of Moab to the top of Pisgah, across from Jericho. There the Lord showed him the whole land—from Gilead to Dan, all of Naphtali, the territory of Ephraim and Manasseh, all the land of Judah as far as the Mediterranean Sea, the Negev and the whole region from the Valley of Jericho, the City of Palms, as far as Zoar... And Moses the servant of the Lord died there in Moab, as the Lord had said. He buried him in Moab, in the valley opposite Beth Peor, but to this day no one knows where his grave is" (Deuteronomy 34:1-4, 6).

What was Moses' response? Acceptance.

Moses could have refused to climb the mountain to look at the land. He could have forced his way into the land. But instead, he did what he was told. And after he climbed the mountain and took in the land with his own eyes, he descended back into the valley and died. And guess who buried him? God.

Yep, the One and only.

Feel free to go back and reread verse 6. I'm not making that up.

Moses accepted God's no, and God tenderly buried him. After Moses viewed the land, he left to go be with the Lord. He didn't rest in the Promised Land. He rested with God Himself.

Acceptance was his final act.

<u>David: Worship</u>

Second Samuel 11 tells the horrid tale of King David's domino-effect of sin. First, he committed adultery with Bathsheba. Then, a baby was conceived. He tried to cover it up by bringing the woman's husband home from war, hoping... well, you know... hoping some intimacy would allow the husband to appear to be the father. When that didn't work, David had the poor man killed in battle, creating the illusion he was a casualty of war. And then he married Bathsheba.

David may have fooled others, but not God. The prophet Nathan confronted him, and David's response was remorse. He had sinned against God, first and foremost, and he owned up to his tragic mistakes (2 Samuel 12:1-13). This was Nathan's response:

"Nathan replied, 'The Lord has taken away your sin. You are not going to die. But because by doing this you have shown utter contempt for the Lord, the son born to you will die'" (2 Samuel 12:13-14).

The child soon became ill. David "pleaded with God for the child. He fasted and spent the nights lying in sackcloth on the ground" (2 Samuel 12:16). After seven days, the child died. The servants were afraid to tell David that he had not survived. David noticed them whispering and shifting uncomfortably, so he pointedly asked if the child was dead. They reluctantly shared the news.

"Then David got up from the ground. After he had washed, put on lotions and changed his clothes, he went into the house of the Lord and worshiped. Then he went to his own house, and at his request they served him food, and he ate" (2 Samuel 12:20).

The servants were perplexed. How did David go from begging God to save the child to worshiping Him after the child died? David reasoned he had done all he could do, and now it was time to move on (2 Samuel 12:22-23). He acknowledged the consequences of his tragic decisions by recognizing God's authority in his life.

Worship was David's first response to God saying no.

The Demon-Possessed Man: Obedience

This man had been tortured by demons for so long that he had been banished to the local cemetery. He could not control his outbursts and, as a result, people were afraid of him. "Night and day he would cry out and cut himself with stones" (Mark 5:5).

The man was miserable.

Jesus entered the scene via a quick boat ride across the lake. The man immediately ran to Jesus and bowed down. Jesus called the demons out of him and put an end to his mental and psychological torture.

Afterwards, the townspeople gathered and found him "dressed and in his right mind" (Mark 5:15). The people could tell immediately that the man had been healed.

Can I make a side note here?

Jesus clothed the man. I don't know if He had a spare outfit or made clothes appear, but He took care to cover his naked body. He not only removed the man's shame, He restored his dignity.

So kind.

So, so kind.

Back to the main point.

As Jesus began to leave, the man begged to go with Him. Maybe he wanted to get away from the townspeople who had banished him for so long. Or perhaps he just wanted to stay close to the One who had rescued him from his mental misery. I tend to think it was the latter. But either way, Jesus said no. He told him to go back to his people and tell of all the wonderful things that had happened in his life.

Do you know what the man did?

He went to the Decapolis—which, by the way, was not a city. It was a term that referred to ten cities. The Decapolis was a region. The man went everywhere telling everyone about Jesus.

This man responded to a "no" with obedience.

Paul: Delight

Paul was radically converted to Christ. He went from persecuting Christians to becoming one himself. His story is a perfect 180-degree transformation. If you aren't familiar with his tale, read Acts 9.

After converting to Christianity, Paul walked intimately with the Lord and was passionate about knowing Him, living for Him, and being willing to die for Him. This man was sold out to Christ on every level.

In 2 Corinthians 12:7, we read about a "thorn in his flesh." Paul describes it as "a messenger from Satan sent to torment him." Scholars differ on what it was: a physical ailment, a chronic illness, a spiritual or psychological issue, or possibly even persecution from others. But everyone agrees it was something rather unpleasant, and Paul did not like it.

Paul asked God three different times to remove it. God denied his request but did so with more than just a no. He explained why.

"But he (God) said to me, 'My grace is sufficient for you, for my power is made perfect in weakness'" (2 Corinthians 12:9).

Here, God states the reason. He told Paul no because this thorn displayed His power. The thorn revealed a weakness in Paul, and that weakness revealed a strength in God.

Now, if this were me, I would not take kindly to it. I don't want to be weak. And I certainly don't want my weaknesses on display. But, as I mentioned before, God didn't choose to memorialize my story in Scripture. He chose to have Paul's story documented because He wants us to learn from Paul. Let's read Paul's response:

"Therefore I will boast all the more gladly about my weaknesses, so that Christ's power may rest on me. That is why, for Christ's sake, I delight in weaknesses, in insults, in hardships, in persecutions, in difficulties. For when I am weak, then I am strong" (2 Corinthians 12:9-10).

Astonishingly, Paul responded with delight.

Initially, he wanted God to remove his thorn, but after God said no, his heart changed. He was now thrilled to have weaknesses and couldn't wait to find more!

Good grief. My knee-jerk response to my own weaknesses could not be further from this.

Once Paul was denied his request, his entire heart changed. He could have been disappointed. He could have been mad. But no.

Paul's response was to delight in the very thing he wanted removed.

Acceptance, worship, obedience, and delight. Four biblical responses to when God says no. Four responses that look terribly difficult on paper. How did they do this? How do we do this today? I mentioned there was a common thread connecting these biblical characters. Here it is:

They viewed God as bigger than themselves.

God was not their equal. In his letter to the church in Phillipi, Paul speaks of Jesus as someone "who did not count equality with God as something to be grasped" (Philippians 2:6). Jesus alone can claim equality with God, yet He chose not to do so.

And yet, aren't we guilty of trying to do just that?

We expect certain things out of life. We expect certain things from God. We respond to a no from Him as if He were some other significant relationship in our lives. When other people say no to us, we can easily take offense. We might ask ourselves: Are they being selfish? Is there a hidden motive or agenda lurking underneath? Who are they to say no to us!

And without realizing it, we sometimes have the same response to God.

We must counsel our own hearts with this truth: His ways are higher than ours. He is holy. His motives are pure. He knows our past, present, and future and how they best fit together. Some promises we must welcome from a distance, the fulfillment of these promises going beyond our lifetime to include others. There is a bigger picture. Making Himself known is paramount. His plans are always, always for our good.

God is not like us. We must never view Him as our equal. Yet we do.

God notes this in us in Psalm 50:21: "You thought I was exactly like you."

We are not exactly like Him. Far from it.

Far, far from it.

God is bigger than us. His authority is over us. That is why Moses responded with acceptance. He respected the decision, though I can't imagine he liked it. After all, he spent 40 years leading quite a contrary group of people throughout the desert. Being denied entrance was heartbreaking. Disappointing! But Moses knew he was not equal to God.

The same goes for David. David wanted his innocent child to live. He begged God to save the baby, but in the end, he respected God's decision and chose to worship Him. Why? Because David knew he was not equal to God.

The man who was demon-possessed willingly obeyed Jesus because he knew the miracle in his life was not because of anything he had done. It was the power of God. He had witnessed the extraordinary presence of God and knew without a doubt that there was no comparison.

And then there is Paul. When he learned that his weakness had the power to show off God's strength, he immediately wanted it to be so in his life. Paul wanted his weaknesses to parade forward on full display for all to see! He understood the inequality and took great delight in allowing it to be magnified in him.

Our current culture does not respect authority. And we are human equals with one another! If we don't like or agree with someone who is over us, we simply ignore them, disobey them, or outright cancel them. Young people struggle to respect grandparents. Adults refuse to comply with the law. Students choose whether or not to respect their teachers. And then there is governmental authority, which holds little to no weight anymore. It is no wonder we view God's authority as optional in our lives. We take it under consideration, but if we don't like it, we respond to it as we do other people in authority over us.

"...you thought I was exactly like you" (Psalm 50:21).

God is not our equal.

Let's let that sink in.

If we can reorient our minds to remember how vastly different we are from God, then might we begin to respond to a "no" from Him with acceptance? With worship? With obedience? And possibly even with delight?

Our difficulty stems from our assumption that we can look God in the eye. That is where our expectations of Him first take root.

There is another common thread among these four stories. These men were able to move on with their lives. They didn't continue in angst over their requests being denied. I am sure they wrestled with disappointment at first. But they got there.

Moses didn't fight. He didn't retaliate. His heart rested. And so did his body. After 40 long years in the desert, he was now in the presence of God. Moses was at peace.

David could not bring his son back to life. Yet he went on to serve God and be known as a man after God's own heart. The Book of Psalms testifies to that.

The demon-possessed man wanted to stay

with Jesus but chose to use his life to tell people about Him. Jesus empowered him, and he obeyed. And his work paved the way for Jesus to later return to the region and be received (Mark 7:31-37).

Paul didn't spend another minute trying to relieve himself of the suffering from the thorn. He turned that thorn into a place of strength. God's power was on display, and he counted that a privilege!

We can respond to a "no" with acceptance, worship, obedience, and delight when we remember God is not our equal. He is holy, majestic, awe-inspiring, powerful, and sovereign. In fact, it is the vastness between us and Him that gives us the grace to accept a "no." Without this incredible inequality, we would be so easily tempted to let anger, disappointment, sorrow, and confusion be our knee-jerk responses. But when we remember who He is and who we are not, it puts our lives in perspective.

What might you need to accept? How can you turn to Him in worship? In what ways do you need to obey? How can you allow what you long to change to become a stepping-stone to more of His strength?

All hard questions.

I don't pretend to assume we can snap our fingers and suddenly respond to a "no" in such admirable ways. This is why maintaining a partnership mentality is so crucial. Trusting He is for us and loves us and is working out great kingdom purposes through us is what enables us to surrender our desires and accept His decision. Remembering we are not equal partners does not devalue our worth but rather greatly increases His. And Scripture speaks for itself. If we want to respond to Him with respect and if we hope to keep moving forward in life when He says no, we must evaluate the way we view ourselves in reference to Him.

It's not easy. But it's possible.

Let's take a step today.

Isaiah 40:25 says, "To whom will you compare me? Or who is my equal? says the Holy One."

Read through the following passage that surrounds this verse, describing our vast inequality to God. Pause after each description, picturing each image as best you can. Ask Him to help you grasp how majestic He is.

"Who has measured the waters in the hollow of his hand, or with the breadth of his hand marked off the heavens?

Who has held the dust of the earth in a basket, or weighed the mountains on the scales and the hills in a balance?

Who can fathom the Spirit of the Lord, or instruct the Lord as his counselor?

Whom did the Lord consult to enlighten him, and who taught him the right way?

Who was it that taught him knowledge or showed him the path of understanding?

With whom, then, will you compare God? To what image will you liken him?

Lift up your eyes and look to the heavens: who created all these?

He who brings out the starry host one by one and calls forth each of them by name.

Because of his great power and mighty strength, not one of them is missing" (Isaiah 40:12-14, 18, 26).

What thoughts or images naturally come to mind when you read these descriptions? Record them in the margins of this page. Take time to praise Him for who He is. Then ask God to help you view your waiting season or an answer of "no" through the lens of His greatness. Consider journaling your experience with this passage and your time in prayer.

We know why God says no. The harder question to answer is how we should respond to it.

May we respond to Him with all the worth and admiration He deserves.

Chapter Twelve
When There Is No Bow

I love a beautifully wrapped package. One with sharp, clean lines on the corners and topped with a bow that is perfectly proportional to the size of the gift. It is so satisfying to finish it and admire my work. And not surprisingly, I don't just prefer this gift-wrapped look with presents, but I also like it in real life.

I like bows. I long to button up the challenging seasons of my life and know there was something significant gained through the hardship. I want to know it was worth it. A lesson was learned. There was beauty involved.

I think we all feel this way, don't we?

But sometimes we can't attach the bow.

We might have it in one hand, hoping to be able to fasten it securely in place. But we just can't put it on... not yet. Or ever.

What do we do when there is no bow?

I have shared numerous stories throughout this book that have bows on them. I have walked through lengthy, very significant in-betweens as well as short, less significant stories in which God taught me a lesson or did something in my heart. A lot of my stories have a bow. That is what makes them easy to tell. Who wants to hear a story without a good ending?

But I also have experiences that don't have bows on them. Relationships that are still a work in progress. Wounds that still need healing. Prayers for loved ones that are yet to be answered. These stories are left untold in this book out of respect for others or because of their own personal nature. I am prepared (or trying to prepare) for these areas not to have the storybook ending I hope for.

We live in a broken world—a world with lots of unfinished stories and sloppily wrapped boxes. So, is there hope for our stories that don't yet have a bow? Ones that might never have one in our lifetime?

Yes, there is.

I am so glad you asked.

The Israelites experienced the weariness of a long wait. After many years of disobedience to God's laws, they were invaded, captured, and taken into captivity by the Babylonians. For seventy years, they lived as exiles, wondering if the bow would ever come. At the point when their strength, faith, and hope in God were waning, the prophet Isaiah addressed them with these words:

"Why do you say, O Jacob, and speak, O Israel, 'My way is hidden from the Lord, and my right is disregarded by my God'? Have you not known? Have you not heard? The Lord is the everlasting God, the Creator of the ends of the earth. He does not faint or grow weary; his understanding is unsearchable" (Isaiah 40: 27-28, ESV).

Suffering had shaped their perspective on life and their view of their Creator. By zeroing in on their difficulties, they had lost sight of God's sovereignty and strength. Isaiah wanted to encourage those who were discouraged, downtrodden, and running on fumes. So continuing in this passage, the prophet showers them with hope. He infuses them with life-giving words designed to buoy their drowning hearts.

"He gives power to the faint, and to him who has no might he increases strength. Even youths shall faint and be weary, and young men shall fall exhausted; but they who wait for the Lord shall renew their strength; they shall mount up with wings like eagles; they shall run and not be weary; they shall walk and not faint" (Isaiah 40:29-31, ESV).

There are so many gems to unpack in this passage, but let's start with the one that is most foundational:

This renewal—this ability to run, and even soar—is not the result of a bow.

It was not because the season ended, or the trial was over that they could finally draw strength from God. This renewed hope was available in advance. They could tap into this hope when they needed it. And the text clearly states how to access it.

"... they who wait for the Lord shall renew their strength..." (v.31).

This word *wait* is translated from the Hebrew word *qavah* which means "to wait expectantly." It might be a little word but it is packed with instruction and insight. The root *qav*, is a noun that means "cord." So the verb form, *qavah*, creates the image of a cord being stretched. A tension—a pulling—a waiting that involves anticipation.

I see this every day with my puppy, Barkley. Because he isn't fully potty trained, we don't let him roam about the house. He has a kennel that opens up to a small fenced-in area. So he can exit the cage but cannot go more than a few steps beyond that. He is quite content in his home within our home.

Until the garage door opens.

As soon as he hears that sound, he darts out of the kennel and walks his paws up the fence until they peek over the top of it. He doesn't bark. Rather, he squeaks with anticipation. He knows he is less than a minute away from human interaction, and he bounces up and down like a pogo stick, eagerly awaiting the arrival of a family member.

That is *qavah*.

It is an eager anticipation of hope. It is a confidence in knowing that hope is pulling in the garage and about to enter in.

But this is where it gets tricky.

Too often we intently wait for our circumstances to change. We tell ourselves that our weariness and exhaustion cannot be renewed until our situation is remedied. We bounce like a puppy in anticipation of having our longings fulfilled. But this verse is crystal clear: Renewed strength is given to those who wait on the Lord, not on circumstances that change.

So what does it mean to wait on the Lord?

Waiting on God involves a posture of remembrance. We wait on Him because we expect Him to act. And we are confident He will act, because we have seen Him act before. But we don't wait on Him for what He will do or to get what we want.

We wait on *Him*. We wait on who He is.

Period.

Isaiah wanted the Israelites to remember God's strength—how He delivered them from Egypt by parting the Red Sea. He wanted them to recall God's faithfulness—how manna was delivered every morning without fail. He wanted them to keep God's protection, kindness, and sovereignty at the forefront of their minds. Their focus was on captivity, suffering, and a longing to go home. Isaiah wanted to redirect their attention.

Isaiah addressed these weary exiles in verse 28: "Have you not known? Have you not heard? The Lord is the everlasting God, the Creator of the ends of the earth. He does not faint or grow weary; his understanding is unsearchable."

In other words, don't forget who God is. Don't forget what you have known. Don't forget what you have heard. Comfort is rooted in His past faithfulness. Faith is believing He will do it again.

In 2017, our house flooded during Hurricane Harvey, forcing us to relocate for seven months. One day, a couple of weeks into that experience, I was overwhelmed and crying. My son, who was in third grade at the time, sat down next to me and said with absolute confidence, "Mom, God is going to take care of us. Remember that hard thing He brought us through last year? He is going to do the same this year."

Do you know what that remembrance did? It refreshed me, renewed my hope, and lifted my spirits. I was deeply encouraged. My son had waited on the Lord by remembering His past faithfulness. In his mind, he eagerly anticipated what he knew God could do, and it strengthened him. And he shared that strength with me. He had nothing physical to offer me as a third grader, but he reminded me to wait on God, knowing He was all I needed.

If we want to move forward in our in-between with hope, we must activate our memories. I love how one particular Bible Project video explains this truth:

"Biblical hope isn't optimism based on the odds, it is a choice to wait on God to bring about a future as surprising as a crucified man rising from the dead. Christian hope looks back to the risen Jesus in order to look forward."[2]

When we wait on God, we remember who He is and what we are confident He can do. For example, we wait on Him to be faithful by not expecting a certain outcome, but rather just knowing He will come through. We wait on Him to provide, trusting it will be exactly what we need. We wait on Him to overcome, confident He is stronger than the enemy. And the list goes on.

To *qavah* on God is to hear the garage door opening and know love, faithfulness, provision, compassion, might, and power are entering in. That is hope. It may surprise you how God's characteristics will manifest themselves in your circumstances, but we can be confident that when we dwell on His nature from the past, it will renew our strength for today.

Here's a quick example of this.

In chapter 2, I shared with you how I became a Christian in college. Prior to that point in time, I didn't know much about Christianity.

In high school, I had a friend named Chris who was active in his church youth group. On several occasions, he invited me to attend, but I always said no. I had no idea what youth group was, so I wasn't interested.

One day, he asked me a pointed question: "Jen, are you a Christian?"

I shrugged and said, "Sure. Isn't everyone in America a Christian?"

That is what I really thought! At that time, I didn't know you had to make a decision to be a Christian.

Now fast-forward to my sophomore year in college. Somewhere in those early months as a believer, I remembered that conversation with Chris. It hit me! I finally understood what he was asking me! He wanted to know if I had made the decision to follow Christ.

When Waiting Feels Like Withholding

Suddenly, I wanted another chance to answer him. I wanted to tell him, "I get what you were asking me now!" I was eager to find him.

The problem was I had no idea where he was.

This was before the internet or social media, and I hadn't seen him in a couple of years. I was also now in college several states away. I had no clue where to begin. My new college friends, however, suggested I pray.

I was new to this and still felt awkward doing it. But I remember sitting on my bed and saying, "God, please help me find Chris. I want to tell him I understand his question now."

That was it. No fanfare. No big churchy words. Just a simple request.

The next morning, my mom, who lived hundreds of miles away and knew nothing about my prayer, went to work. That day she was working at a hotel in Lexington, Kentucky, about an hour away from her home. She donned her nametag and took her place behind the counter.

In walked Chris.

He didn't know my mom but went to her for assistance and noted her name tag. He said, "I knew a girl in high school with that last name. Are you related to someone named Jen?"

My mom nodded enthusiastically. After a brief exchange, Chris wrote down his phone number and asked her to give it to me. He was eager to know how I was doing! I cannot begin to tell you how shocked I was when my mom called me that afternoon.

Less than 24 hours after my prayer, I had Chris' phone number scribbled on a notepad in my room.

To this day, I think about that answered prayer. Some of the situations in my life that don't have bows on them yet involve unanswered prayers. And at times, I grow weary. I get discouraged. I wonder if God hears me. I wonder if He is big enough to answer.

And then I remembered the moment I got Chris' phone number.

That one experience taught me that God hears me and that He is powerful. It also demonstrated how much He loves me. If He cared about that tiny detail in my life, how much more would He care about the bigger ones?

To wait on Him means I remember how powerful He was in answering that prayer. Recalling His might and ability to line up my circumstances (and my mom's and Chris'!) energizes me. It doesn't take long to renew my hope and strengthen my resolve to keep praying. I can go from feeling discouraged to soaring when I remind myself of God's ability to act.

That is the power of waiting on God.

I have been drawing strength from God's power and provision from that prayer for years. But recently, God has given me another reason to wait on Him.

I shared with you earlier in the book my desire first for a speaking career and later for a writing career. After almost 20 years of trying, I was ready to give up.

As I was making the mental decision to surrender this once and for all, I got an email from a women's organization. The subject line was: Do you have a book idea but don't know what to do with it? I tentatively opened the email. The organization was touting a ten-week training designed to help authors turn ideas into book proposals and eventually published works. It required a lengthy application and a writing sample of my book idea.

I sat with the email for several days. Should I attempt to pursue this? In the end, I decided to throw my name in the hat. I trusted that if the door shut on this, then the door was shutting forever.

No one was more surprised than I was to receive the email saying I had been accepted. Hope was rekindled! I was sure God was in it.

I wanted to write a book about waiting. It had been such a theme in my life! As I worked on several sample chapters, I remember the day I wrote this sentence: "My waiting felt like God was withholding from me." I was sitting on my soft, cherry-red couch with my legs tucked underneath me and my laptop perched on top. I stopped typing immediately and stared at the words.

When waiting feels like withholding...

Everything about how I felt was captured in that one phrase. It was my journey wrapped up in five words.

For the remaining weeks, I worked long and hard, and when the training was over, I held my breath. What would happen now?

The news could not have been more disappointing. The final feedback contained some painful comments that left me feeling defeated. I was lacking an agent, a robust social media presence and I was told this book didn't have a future in its current state. But its current state was my life, so I had reached a dead end. I decided it was indeed time to stop pursuing a career that had no hope of materializing. After 20 years, I put it all to rest.

Several months went by, however, and I still found myself longing to write. I couldn't turn off how I was naturally wired. Then one day, a random idea struck me: *I wonder if I could write a magazine article?* I don't need an agent or social media followers to do that! And unlike a speaking opportunity, I don't have to be invited to submit an article.

I Googled how to write for a woman's magazine and took a stab at it. I wrote an article about perseverance and a few weeks later, got an email saying it had been accepted! I remember when the magazine arrived in my mailbox. I couldn't believe it.

So I submitted another one. And another one after that. I searched for magazines that fit my style and began sending in submissions. Some were rejected, and some were accepted. But I enjoyed the process. I was no longer striving for something more. There was no pressure. Magazine articles became my thing.

And then one day, five years later, I went to a funeral.

A woman named Beth spotted me and came over to say hello. I had met Beth briefly during that ten-week training five years earlier but had not seen her since. She was also a writer.

After exchanging hellos, she asked me what book ideas I was working on. I told her I was no longer pursuing a book and instead I was writing for magazines. She proceeded to invite me to a coffee shop where a group of writers gathered every month to share their book-writing journeys and encourage one another. I reminded her again; I was not currently writing a book and wasn't planning to. She was undeterred and continued to invite me.

The interaction was so unexpected, it piqued my curiosity. So, I decided to go.

That Friday morning, I gathered around a table with seven other women. True to Beth's description, they each took a turn sharing what they were writing. They encouraged each other and offered feedback. I spoke last.

I felt silly because I didn't have a project I was working on. So, I was honest and told them I had an idea, but it was five years old and I had not touched it since.

"What is it about?" one of the writers asked.

I stated the title: *When Waiting Feels Like Withholding.*

Before I had a chance to further explain it, the group began making comments and noting how they had felt that way in their lives.

One of the women, seated catty-corner to me, spoke up next.

"I might be interested in a book like that." I learned then that she was a writer *and* a publisher.

I was stunned.

We exchanged contact information, and

made arrangements to meet two weeks later in her home. That day, sitting in her living room, she opened our time together with this statement: "Before we discuss anything today, I want you to know I am extending you a book contract."

I was speechless.

I stumbled through a couple of questions. Don't I need a book proposal? An agent? More of a social media platform than my paltry excuse of one?

She responded by explaining that normally, yes, those are important, but that my situation was different. She said she was praying and felt like God told her to offer me a contract on faith.

Tears welled up in my eyes. I had completely put this dream to bed and could not believe that, in a matter of two weeks, it was suddenly wide-awake again. With someone I had only met briefly in a coffee shop!

If that were the entire story, it would be good, but it actually gets better.

As I began working on this book, I pulled up all the sample chapters I had written five years ago and knew I had major changes to make. My story had evolved and so had my walk with God. I was not the same person. As I began rewriting the first chapter with a new angle, I remembered I had written an article on that topic a few years back. I pulled it up on my laptop and knew that with a few changes, and a bit more content, this article could become the chapter.

When I finished that chapter, the next one naturally emerged in my mind. That topic too, was an article I had previously written. So, I updated and revised that article into a chapter.

The same thing happened again. And again.

Out of the 13 chapters in this book, nine of them are previously written articles.

As this book began to take shape, it hit me. I had been writing this book for five years—I just didn't know it.

I had grieved over this dream. And God had been strangely quiet. Silent, in fact. He had let me pine after a career (that morphed into wanting to write a book) for years and then let me surrender it without fanfare. The only leading I had ever felt from God all these years was the desire to teach. Other than that, nothing. I had always wondered why He had let me walk this road for so long only to have it come to an abrupt and painful end five years ago.

Had I gone through all of that just to be content writing for magazines? Maybe? But gosh, couldn't there have been an easier way to get to this point?

But as I wrote the book you now hold in your hands, I realized He had been there all along. I just couldn't see it. He *did* have plans for me. I just didn't know them yet.

These articles were not originally about waiting. They were about feeling forgotten, not understanding God's ways, battling fear, and persevering one day at a time. But once I threaded my needle with waiting, I was able to sew them all together into one train of thought. Only God could have me write a book right under my own nose!

Now I realize this story has a bow. My desires ended in a published book, and I couldn't be more thrilled. But aren't we talking about not having bows? And might this story seem trite in comparison to those with a chronic illness, infertility, or a deeply struggling child?

Why do I share this story with you?

This book journey has built my faith in the areas of my life where I still don't see God at work. Where there is no bow. Where silence prevails. In the places where my prayers are still unanswered.

This bow allows me to wait on God, knowing even when I think He's silent, He's not. Even when I think He has forgotten me, He hasn't. And even when I think He doesn't care, He does. I can now look at the areas of my life that are not neatly wrapped up and know God is very much in the messiness of them.

As I mentioned at the beginning of this

chapter, I still have relationships that are a work in progress, wounds that need healing, and prayers for loved ones that are not yet answered. But instead of letting uncertainty or fear or doubt get the best of me, I can combat those thoughts with the very real work of God in my life with this book.

God is at work in each area of my life where my heart still longs for something. I don't have to see it in my circumstances to know He is present in them. This book is my living proof of that.

So, yes, a book contract is certainly trite in comparison to more pressing life issues, but the sovereignty of God is the same in both. Once you have witnessed the power of God in your life, you can apply it to any and all situations. And *that* is how we take comfort in our bow-less situations.

Make no mistake, friends. Just because you can't see God at work in your waiting doesn't mean He isn't there. If He was faithful before, He will be faithful again. So, take a moment to remember. To wait on Him.

To *qavah*.

List out His faithfulness in your situation. Record His provision. Journal when you have witnessed His compassion, experienced His love, marveled at His might. Ask Him to give you eyes to see *Him* in your circumstances and how He has protected you throughout. Once you chronicle these treasures, read them over and over again. Let His power and provision and protection be your focus.

Wait on Him.

Not your circumstances.

I don't need a bow to overcome my weariness in the in-between. I need to wait on Him, knowing He has never left my side—and never will. I don't need my current circumstances to confirm His presence in my life. I need to remember all He has done and let those memories infuse my mind and build my faith. In looking back, I am able to move forward.

As I wait on Him, He will renew my strength. I will mount up on wings like an eagle. I will run and not grow weary. I will walk and not grow faint.

And so can you, my friend.

So can you.

Chapter Thirteen
The (Real) End

When my younger son was four years old, he asked to say the blessing at dinner. He carefully interlaced his fingers, squeezed his eyes shut and said, "Dear Jesus, thank you for this food and can I please die tonight so I can be with you in heaven?" Utterly shocked, I shot off my own prayer like an emergency flare begging Jesus not to answer him.

My son's life had not been filled with heartache and tragedy, causing him to long for it to be over. After all, he was only four! Rather, he had learned about heaven and quickly surmised that living there had to be better than living here. So why wait?

For years now, I have wrestled with my reaction to his prayer. Why was I so quick to thwart it? If heaven is as amazing as Scripture describes, why wouldn't I want him to be there? The simple answer is this: I have made this place my home, and I don't want him to leave it. Maybe he wanted to go to heaven that night, but I wanted him to stay.

Hebrews 11 reminds me that I am a stranger and an alien here on earth (v.13). Like Abraham, I am to live as a nomad, "looking forward to the city with foundations, whose architect and builder is God" (v.10). But instead, I have settled in a place where the architect and builder is man.

Heaven is a place fully constructed by God. Nothing man-made. Can you imagine how magnificent it will be? Marvel with me for a minute about our earthly home. Consider a striking sunset or a majestic mountaintop. Ponder a rugged redwood or a beautiful beach. Picture a batch of colorful coral pulsing to the beat of the ocean. Now let your imagination begin to swell to include the glorious possibilities of heaven. Make no mistake, heaven will be beyond beautiful. I expect to be speechless upon arrival.

So why don't I ache to be there now?

Well, in all honesty, I do ache for heaven—when life on earth isn't going according to plan. I am not a fan of suffering. I am a wimp when it comes to pain, and sometimes my faith is so weak I just can't fathom how something hard could turn into anything good. And have I mentioned I don't like to wait? There are days that the uncertainty, and all the insecurities and disappointments that stem from that, make me long for eternity.

So yes, I do ache for heaven, but only when this life isn't going well.

Sigh.

But can we wrestle with this for a minute? Instead of beating myself up for only yearning for heaven when I don't like my circumstances on earth, I want to press into how that can change. Let's ponder this question:

How would our season of waiting change if we saw it through the lens of our final destination?

Every day I make decisions based on how I assume my future will unfold. Whether I am excited or dreading what lies ahead, it shapes how I think and act. The level of confidence I have in tomorrow greatly influences how I feel today.

So what if we allowed our forever home in heaven to inform our temporary one here? It seems only fitting to finish this book with a taste of how we know the real story ends. Being confident of where we are headed may not change our circumstances, but it certainly can affect our attitude toward them.

I believe there are at least three ways we can allow eternity to influence us as we wait.

1. Allow suffering to redirect your heart.

We know this is not our home. Deep down, the underlying ache for contentment, the hatred of evil, and the brokenness we see in ourselves and others confirm that there must be something more. Something better. Suffering cries out that this is not our home.

But we often silence the message behind those cries.

Our culture goes to great lengths to avoid any type of hardship. The slightest prick of pain, unease, or boredom is quickly remedied with our drug of choice: distraction. Entertainment—whether it be endless podcasts, binge-worthy dramas, or the drone of social media—keeps the gnawing for something more at bay.

In short, we have learned to numb our eternal longings.

But who can blame our obsession with diversion and pleasure? We are constantly bombarded with messages like YOLO (you only live once) and FOMO (fear of missing out) that urgently call us to "live for today" and "follow your dreams." Essentially, we are told ad nauseum not to set our sights on what's coming because this life is all we have.

Similarly, if we only set our sights on what this life can offer, then this life is all we will want. These mantras have successfully eliminated eternity from the equation of life.

So how do we reawaken our eternal longings? One way is to listen to the cries of suffering that remind us this is not our home. Allow your struggles to redirect your heart to long for and live for eternity.

When I think about our level of comfort and ability to avoid pain, it stands in stark contrast to the apostle Paul. He recounts how he received lashes, was beaten with rods, pelted with stones, and shipwrecked three times. He was in danger from rivers, bandits, Jews, Gentiles, and false believers, in cities, in countries, and at sea. He was hungry and thirsty, cold and naked (2 Corinthians 11:23-27).

When I read that passage, I am quick to note the gratitude in my heart. I am so thankful that isn't my story! I want to love Jesus yet still live comfortably. Even one of those hardships feels like more than I can handle. So, it's easy for me to look at Paul's life with pity. But I bet if Paul were here today, he would pity mine. He knows I am missing out if I don't grasp what it's like to truly long for eternity and live my life based on that desire. If I am content with my life here, or if I only set my sights on the achievements, accolades, and comforts of this world, then I don't know the joy of aching for what is to come.

When Waiting Feels Like Withholding

Paul and the early church lived with persecution and could not numb the pain. They had every reason to want to exit this life and be done with it. Instead, they used their discomfort to redirect their hearts toward eternity. They allowed suffering to motivate them to make every day count for God (more on this in the next section). But with our lack of persecution and increase of comfort and entertainment, it is much easier to settle in and try (unsuccessfully) to make this our home.

But what if we used frustration or disappointment to our own spiritual advantage? What if we allowed our suffering to ignite a longing for eternity within us? Could we channel our angst in prayer instead of numbing it with distraction? Psalm 62:8 tells us to "pour out our hearts to him, for God is our refuge."

Recently, I have been learning the benefit of doing this.

A few months back, I had a heartbreaking experience with someone and was crushed by our interaction. At first, I wanted to reach out to a friend, knowing she would offer the comfort I craved, but I decided to turn only to God. I cried and prayed and told Him everything I was feeling. I poured out my heart until there wasn't a drop left. I had no idea how to change my situation and told Him that.

A couple of days later, I was dumbfounded

by a phone call I received that moved this situation in a positive direction. Some of the words spoken to me were the very words I had prayed about. It was unmistakably an answered prayer. God had intervened in my life over an issue that only He knew about! I was instantly reminded that my faith is real, and that God is personally involved in my life.

There is value in pouring out our hearts to Him. Those intimate interactions with God serve to increase my longing to be with Him. When He meets me in my pain with peace, I long to be with the Prince of Peace. Our suffering is not in vain when we use it to pivot our perspective back toward heaven and draw near to Him. Suffering can redirect our hearts toward eternal longings.

And it can diminish our earthly ones.

In his book *Living Life Backwards*, David Gibson says, "People who follow Jesus often lose sight of the world to come. We become residents rather than nomads. We become fully integrated in this world rather than viewing ourselves as passing through and we do this by living as if our greatest treasures are here and now...We hold the good things of this world too tightly and lavish our affections on them too freely."[3]

Might the pain of the in-between lessen if we weren't so attached to the things of this world and the goals we hope to achieve? Similarly, what if we allowed the disappointments of this life to channel our longings to where we will be fully satisfied?

In other words, what if we viewed suffering as a warning light on the dashboard of our hearts? A signal that we need to reassess our priorities or consider how much we expect something to satisfy. Try thinking through the following questions:

Is the pain of your in-between a result of an earthly treasure you assume you can't live without? Examine the root of your frustration or disappointment. Does it stem from your attempts to make this life the only one worth living? Is there anything you need to loosen your grip upon?

If we can allow suffering to redirect our hearts toward heaven and away from earthly treasures, we create space for an eternal perspective to infiltrate our thinking and shape our seasons of waiting. Don't be quick to numb your trials with distraction. Rather, let the pain cause you to yearn for heaven and nudge your heart away from what can never fully satisfy.

2. Stop living for yourself

Let's be honest. How do we live fully present here on earth but not make this our home?

I don't think God wants us clinging so tightly to our earthly dreams and desires that we lose our longing for heaven. But He also doesn't want us to be so miserable here that we long to leave. So again, how do we reside here with a temporary mindset? How do we long for heaven without being miserable on earth?

It's a fine line. A delicate dance. A constant tension.

In 2 Corinthians 5, Paul reminds us of Jesus' sacrifice and then states that "he died for all, that those who live should no longer live for themselves but for him who died for them and was raised for them" (v. 15).

We should no longer live for ourselves.

Therein lies the fine line, the dance, the tension. The more we live for ourselves, the more eternity fades into the background.

Paul further reiterates this a few verses later. "We are therefore Christ's ambassadors, as though God were making his appeal through us. We implore you on Christ's behalf: Be reconciled to God" (v. 20).

God wants us to live for Him as an ambassador. He wants to make His appeal to others through us.

Please don't rush past that.

Have you ever been used by God in someone else's life? It is a privilege. A joy! God's hope for us is not that we would make this our home, but that we would live for Him and allow that calling to satisfy our hearts. Home is coming. For now, let your life and your circumstances be a vessel for Him to work through you.

Remember, an ambassador is one who lives in a country not their own for the sole purpose of representing the country that is their own. An ambassador represents the king, speaks for the king, and makes decisions based on the king. The agenda of an ambassador is based on the agenda of the king. But all the while the ambassador knows this country is not their home.

As Christians, we step into the role of an ambassador the moment we give our lives to Jesus. We don't apply for, aspire to, or try to earn this title. Rather, we receive the job on the spot. No resume required (2 Corinthians 5:17). How great is that? This role is not a burden, but a privilege. Adopting and maintaining an ambassador mindset is critical for followers of Christ, especially in the in-between. It is at the heart of our partnership with Him.

Imagine for a moment how different your life would be if you saw it through the lens of this unique role. Consider a current relational conflict you have. How would your level of patience, compassion, or frustration change if you viewed yourself as someone who no longer lived for yourself and instead saw yourself as a messenger for Christ?

Now, consider your season of waiting. How does living like an ambassador change the way you view this season? How might God be using you to point others to Him? How could your patience, faithfulness, or trust in God make an eternal impact on others? When we no longer live for ourselves but for Him who died for us, it empowers us in our role as an ambassador and sets our sights on eternity.

3. Use the end of the story to your advantage.

Confusion can wreak havoc in our lives if we are not careful. And never was there more confusion in Scripture than in the time between the death and resurrection of Jesus. In all four gospel accounts, we find Jesus' followers spiritually hunched over in a puzzled posture, trying to make sense of the fact that Jesus died on the cross right before their eyes. As readers, we skip over their confusion. We know the end of the story, so we bypass the hours that left people wandering in their thoughts.

But let's take a moment and sit with them. What was it like for them the morning of the resurrection?

Mary Magdalene and a few other women arrived at the tomb with spices to anoint Jesus' body. They fully expected Jesus to be dead. (Otherwise, they would have left the spices at home.) Finding the tomb empty left them "trembling and bewildered" (Mark 16:8).

Mary hurried to find Peter and tell him Jesus' body was missing. Peter raced to the tomb and "bending over, he saw the strips of linen lying by themselves, and he went away, wondering to himself what had happened" (Luke 24:12).

Trembling, bewildered, wondering.

Everything they thought they knew and understood was turned upside down. Now, please resist the urge to jump to the end of the story. Instead, imagine yourself at the tomb. Allow yourself to be perplexed, unsure, troubled or even scared. Can you feel their grief as they try to process everything that transpired over the past three days? It was one thing to witness His death, but now they were thrown into a whole new sphere of emotions.

Where was His body?

I can only imagine how excruciating those hours were. Hope had been snuffed out like a candle and now even the candle was gone.

When I read the gospel accounts of the resurrection with the end in mind, I want to cry out to Mary and Peter, "Hang on! Jesus is coming!" I know Jesus is about to call Mary by name and stand before the disciples, greeting them with peace (John 20:16,19). I want to share the good news with them — that joy is just around the corner. Their grief has an expiration date.

Knowing the end of the story changes the way I read it.

So why can't I do the same thing with my life today?

When I think of my in-betweens in light of my entire life, I picture it like a jigsaw puzzle. One portion of the puzzle looks fully formed, while another section is missing a piece or several pieces, creating either a tiny or a gaping open space. But what I am learning is that those pieces aren't really missing. Rather, they are just invisible to me at the moment. The puzzle has been and always will be complete (Psalm 139:16).

Mary Magdalene didn't recognize Jesus when He first stood before her at the empty tomb (John 20:14). The two men en route to Emmaus were joined by Jesus on their journey, yet they didn't realize it was Him (Luke 24:15-16). Jesus Himself told the disciples He would die and be raised three days later, yet Peter and John, on the morning of the resurrection, "still did not understand from Scripture that Jesus had to rise from the dead" (John 20:9).

The puzzle pieces were always there; they just couldn't see them.

Just as I want to cry out to Mary and Peter to hang on, I know the "great cloud of witnesses" in Hebrews 12:1 is cheering me on. They are exclaiming, "Hang on, Jen!

The puzzle is complete, you just can't see it."

And they are calling out to you, too.

"Hang on, __(your name)__! The puzzle is complete, you just can't see it."

Mary and Peter didn't know the end of the story that morning. They were living in real time. But we do! So let's use it to our advantage. Even if your situation looks as bleak as that first Easter morning, with Jesus nowhere in sight, remember the end. Put your faith in how you know it ends.

The puzzle is complete, you just can't see it.

Hang on, my friend.

Hang on.

Let's consider these three points: if we can allow suffering to redirect our hearts, stop living for ourselves, and use the end of the story to our advantage, we can allow heaven to influence our daily life. And peace will enter in because heaven is where peace reigns.

Sit with me for a moment and imagine the place where this peace reigns. Where contentment and satisfaction are a guarantee. Where endless striving ceases to exist. Where nothing feels withheld because nothing is withheld.

Now picture the One who makes all of that possible.

Take a few minutes to read through this list, comparing what is with what *will be.*

Right now I am hurting, but soon He will be my healing.

Right now I am confused, but soon He will bring clarity.

Right now I am disappointed, but soon He will be my satisfaction.

Right now I am fearful, but soon He will be my peace.

Right now I am broken, but soon He will make me whole.

Right now I am tired, but soon He will give me rest.

Right now I am _____, but soon He will _____.

What would you fill in those blanks? Go ahead. Make your own list.

One day all will be made well. What began in the garden of Eden in Genesis 1 and 2 will be fully restored and forever sealed. But don't forget the good news for today. You can experience glimpses of these beautiful promises now.

We can take refuge in Him when we are scared (Psalm 91:1-6).

When Waiting Feels Like Withholding

We can find our comfort in Him when we are hurting (Psalm 34:18).

We can find rest in Him when we are weary (Matthew 11:28).

We can find our satisfaction in Him when we are longing (Psalm 37:4).

Jesus offers a peace that passes understanding, and it is available to us now (Philippians 4:6-7). God promises wisdom when we ask for it (James 1:5). The Lord loves us more than we can fathom (Romans 5:8) and nothing can separate us from that love (Romans 8:38-39). He is for us, not against us (Romans 8:31), knows the number of hairs on our head (Luke 12:7), and knows us each by name (John 10:3). And God never takes His eyes off of us because He does not sleep (Psalm 121:3-5).

Feeling withheld by God is simply that—a feeling. And it is that feeling that causes us to doubt His goodness and struggle to trust Him. Moving forward, let's take the facts of the Bible and walk by faith. May we be open to God simply protecting us, guiding us, or providing differently for us. May we count it a privilege to be used by Him to make Himself known.

Don't let the longings you have for this earthly life be your ultimate aim. Ask God to help you hold them loosely. Walk the path God has for you, knowing it is paved directly to Him. Allow the emotions wrapped up in your waiting serve to remind you this is not your home and let them fuel your desire to be there. Because soon you will be home. But until then, take up the mantle of the ambassador and use this time for His mission.

Nothing done for the Kingdom of God is ever in vain. In the end, it will be worth it.

So worth it.

One day we will dwell with God. Our faith will become sight. We will be with Him forever, and He will be with us. The apostle John records these words for us in the final book of the Bible:

"I saw the Holy City, the new Jerusalem, coming down out of heaven from God, prepared as a bride beautifully dressed for her husband. And I heard a loud voice from the throne saying, 'Look! God's dwelling place is now among the people, and he will dwell with them. They will be his people, and God himself will be with them and be their God.'" (Revelation 21:2-3).

Reading on in this same passage, we get a glimpse of what Jesus will do first. It is so beautiful.

"He will wipe every tear from their eyes. There will be no more death or mourning or crying or pain, for the old order of things has passed away" (Revelation 21:4).

Can you imagine Jesus wiping your tears?

It is such an intimate act. So personal. So sincere. But it leaves me with a question. Why will I be crying? If we are in a place with no more crying, why will there be tears?

I don't know the answer for certain. Scripture doesn't tell us. But here is what I choose to believe: I think they will be tears of relief. I think when I finally get to heaven, my mind and heart will be so grateful that I won't be able to contain my emotions.

The wait is over.

I'm here.

I'm finally here.

As I stated at the beginning of this chapter, I expect to be speechless when I cross the threshold of eternity, but I don't think it will be because I am somewhere that looks spectacular or feels free. Rather, it will be because I am face to face with the Voice that rescued me and sustained me. The One who comforted me and loved me here on earth. The One who heard my cries and captured every tear in a bottle.

The One who was always with me in the waiting.

Finally.

Jesus.

Author's Note

Shortly before this book went to print, I heard a wonderful message on the woman at the well from John 4. It was titled, "Come See A Man." This biblical story is richly layered with so much beauty and meaning and purpose. In it, Jesus goes out of His way to meet with a Samaritan woman who had a sordid past. His intention was to give her hope. True, life-changing hope. After a brief conversation with Him, the woman is forever changed. She runs away from the well, back into town, eager to tell everyone, "Come see a man…" (John 4:29).

Come see a man who has given me hope!

Come see a man who has changed my life!

The townspeople listened and followed

her back to where Jesus was. As the passage states, "Many of the Samaritans from that town believed in him because of the woman's testimony" (v. 39) and after Jesus stayed two more days we learn that, "because of his words many more people became believers" (v. 41).

And then the townspeople spoke to the woman:

"We no longer believe just because of what you said; now we have heard for ourselves, and we know that this man really is the Savior of the world" (v. 42). In other words, we don't need your words anymore. We have our own now.

Throughout this book, I have eagerly proclaimed:

"Come see a man who was with me in the wait!"

"Come see a man who never stopped caring about me!"

"Come see a man who never forgot me, was never punishing me, and was always in control."

"Come see a man who loves me. A man who loves you too."

My sincere prayer and hope for you is that you can now say, "I don't need your words anymore, Jen. I have my own."

It has been a privilege to journey with you.

Thank you for taking the time to read these words. But now you don't need this book anymore. If you have met Him and met *with* Him then my goal was accomplished. Because the honest truth is this...

All you ever needed was Him anyway.

He is with you in the wait, my friend. And He always will be.

Let me leave you with these final words of hope.

"I remain confident of this: I will see the goodness of the Lord in the land of the living. Wait for the Lord; be strong and take heart and wait for the Lord" (Psalm 27:13-14).

With all my heart,

ACKNOWLEDGEMENTS

Thank you, Elisabeth Cutrer, for poring over these chapters. I think you have read every page of every writing project I have ever attempted, and I am grateful. You've been with me from the start! You are my go-to for feedback, inspiration, and honesty. And you always deliver. Your fingerprints are on every page of this book, and the book is better for it.

Many thanks to Heather Henry. You came in clutch at the end! Your eagle editorial eye brilliantly pulled this project together. Thank you for going the extra mile to see it through to the end. I stand by the fact that a writer is only as good as her editor. Thank you for polishing this up so nicely.

Thank you, Allison Allred, Peggy Bodde, and Amy Lively for being my first readers. You noted everything that wasn't clear theologically and narratively and gave me honest, raw insight into how you received it emotionally. You made the book stronger, and I thank you.

I also want to thank Kevin Mckee for not only reading this and offering feedback, but answering random questions, being a sounding board for ideas, providing research to consider, and most of all for praying that the writing process "would be nothing but joy the whole time." It was!

Thank you, Shelly Esser, for inadvertently helping me write this book. It was a joy and a privilege to write for Just Between Us magazine, and your edits to my original articles shaped so much of what you now hold in your hands. I hope you recognize your work deep within these pages.

Thank you, Lorraine Kennedy, Jennifer Zimmerman, and Wendy TerHaar, for teaching me, modeling for me, and helping me live out the final chapters of this book. I cherish our small group and have tried to soak up every ounce of wisdom you have each poured out.

Thank you, Michelle Jester, and Rope Swing Publishing, for taking a chance on me and trusting God with offering me a book deal. That was truly a beautiful day. And thank you to the additional editors, graphic designers, formatters, and everyone else who put in the work to help me get the book to publish.

And many thanks to Rachea Amdemariam, Alana May and the rest of my launch team for helping me cross the finish line and market this book for all to read. It was fast and furious, but we did it!

I want to give extra thanks to my family. I love you, Aaron and Parker. Thank you for letting me share your stories and for always cheering me on. Dave, year after year you have never stopped believing in me, and I love you for that. Thank you for always being with me in the wait.

Lastly, thank you, Jesus. None of these words would exist without you. You are faithful. May your message speak loud and clear. Do with this book what you will. I'm just along for the ride!

ABOUT THE AUTHOR

Jen's writing journey began in the classroom, where she rewrote Sunday School curriculum to better connect Scripture to everyday life. What started as a simple effort to reach her Sunday school class has grown into blogs, articles, chapter contributions, and a six-week Bible study. Her work has been featured with Proverbs 31 Ministries and in publications such as A Joyful Life and Today's Christian Living. Jen also writes for the Life Bible app and The Truly Co., and she serves as a regular columnist and feature writer for Just Between Us magazine.

For more than 20 years, Jen has taught and spoken to women's ministries, sharing biblical encouragement with warmth and clarity. She holds a Master of Divinity from Southwestern Baptist Theological Seminary and remains a lifelong learner at heart.

Jen is married and the proud mom of two sons, one in college and one on the way. When she is not writing, you will likely find her dreaming about anything that involves a lake. Connect with Jen at @jen_allee_author and jenallee.com.

REFERENCES

1 Scouting the Divine by Margaret Feinberg, p.71

2 www.BibleProject.com/articles/what-does-isaiah-4031-wings-eagles-verse-mean/ ARTICLES/WHAT-DOES-ISAIAH-4031-WINGS-

3 Living Life Backwards by David Gibson, p.36

www.ingramcontent.com/pod-product-compliance
Ingram Content Group UK Ltd.
Pitfield, Milton Keynes, MK11 3LW, UK
UKHW022210230426
12048UKWH00016BA/749